3L6C

SITUATIONAL LEADERSHIP FOR PRINCIPALS

The School Administrator in Action

Other Books by the Authors

Practical Approaches to Individualizing Instruction: Contracts and Other Effective Teaching Strategies (1972)

Educator's Self Teaching Guide to Individualizing Instructional Programs (1975)

Administrator's Guide to New Programs for Faculty Management and Evaluation (1977)

How to Raise Independent and Professionally Successful Daughters (1977)

Teaching Students Through Their Individual Learning Styles: A Practical Approach (1978)

SITUATIONAL LEADERSHIP FOR PRINCIPALS

The School Administrator in Action

Kenneth Dunn, Ed.D. and Rita Dunn, Ed.D.

Illustrations and Jacket Design by Charlotte Kindilien

PRENTICE-HALL, INC.
ENGLEWOOD CLIFFS, NEW JERSEY

Prentice-Hall International, Inc., *London*
Prentice-Hall of Australia, Pty. Ltd., *Sydney*
Prentice-Hall Canada Inc., *Toronto*
Prentice-Hall of India Private Ltd., *New Delhi*
Prentice-Hall of Japan, Inc., *Tokyo*
Prentice-Hall of Southeast Asia Pte. Ltd., *Singapore*
Whitehall Books, Ltd., *Wellington, New Zealand*
Editors Prentice-Hall Do Brasil LTDA., *Rio De Janeiro*

© 1983 by
Prentice-Hall, Inc.
Englewood Cliffs, N.J.

All rights reserved. No part of this book may be reproduced in any form or by any means without permission in writing from the publisher.

Library of Congress Cataloging in Publication Data

Main entry under title:

Situational leadership for principals.

Includes bibliographical references and index.
 1. School management and organization.
 2. School superintendents and principals.
I. Dunn, Kenneth J. II. Dunn, Rita Stafford

LB2801.A1S58 1982   371.2   82-11211
ISBN 0-13-810770-X

Printed in the United States of America

About the Authors

KENNETH J. DUNN has served as a teacher and school administrator, as superintendent of schools at Chappaqua and Hewlitt-Woodmere, New York, and as adjunct professor at both Hunter College and St. John's University. He earned his doctorate at Teachers College, Columbia University, where his thesis was used as a model design for collaborative leadership.

Dr. Dunn is a past executive director of The Education Council for School Research and Development and has been a consultant to many state education departments, school systems, and technical agencies. He is presently professor in the Department of Graduate Programs in Educational Services at Queens College of the City University of New York.

RITA S. DUNN is professor, Division of Administration and Instructional Leadership, St. John's University, New York, where she serves as editor of the Learning Styles Network's *Newsletter* for the Center for the Study of Learning and Teaching Styles. She earned her doctorate at New York University and was awarded the NYU Research Scholarship Award.

In 1980, Dr. Dunn was named "College Teacher of the Year" by the New York Teachers of English Association. In 1981, she was selected for a research professorship at Ohio University's National Center for Research in Vocational Education. In March, 1982, she was named "Outstanding Consultant of the Year" by the Association for Supervision and Curriculum Development at its national convention in Anaheim, California.

The Dunns' combined publications include 6 books and over 150 published articles and research papers in magazines such as *The Kappan, Educational Leadership, NASSP Journal, Learning, Instructor,* and *Early Years.* They received Education Press of America national recognition for their seven-part "Workshop in Print" in *Instructor,* described as "the best series...published in an educational journal in 1977..." Their books include: *Practical Approaches to Individualizing Instruction* (1972), *Educator's Self-Teaching Guide to Individualizing Instructional Programs* (1975), *Administrator's*

Guide to New Programs for Faculty Management and Evaluation (1977), and *Teaching Students Through Their Individual Learning Styles* (1978).

Acknowledgments

It has been our long-standing goal to involve a group of professors of a leading School of Education in the development of a book that would be an "on the job" tool in the hands of practicing school building administrators, as well as those who have been newly appointed. Therefore, we gratefully acknowledge the contributions of the following faculty members of the Division of Administrative and Instructional Leadership and The Division of Human Services and Counseling at St. John's University, Jamaica, New York:

> Zarif Bacilious
> James R. Campbell
> Eugene Geisert
> Josephine Gemake
> Shirley A. Griggs
> Jean Hazelton
> Virginia L. Kavanagh
> William McLaughlin
> William Sanders
> Richard Sinatra
> John Spiridakis
> John Swanchak
> Erika Wick

Each of these University instructors has worked in actual school settings and continues to have direct involvement in the day-to-day problems of practicing teachers, administrators, and those in training in the schools as well as in graduate education programs. This group of knowledgeable professors submitted more than twenty of the situations described in the text; each of the cases, problems, confrontations and memos are based on real events that they either experienced or observed. All of the professor/authors have assisted teachers, administrators and school districts as consultants, supervisors, and/or coordinators.

In addition, situations were solicited from other practicing supervisors and teachers. Several were accepted from the following contributors who served as coauthors:

> Joseph M. Aquino
> Donal F. Buckley
> Carole A. Decker
> Patricia A. Green
> Barbara Shay
> Kathy Shanahan

Dr. Angela Bruno of Akron University also contributed to this text. To each of the above we express our appreciation.

A Word from the Authors

The experienced administrator recognizes that specific problems and situations repeat over and over again. People, relationships and interactions have their counterparts in every school system; indeed, in every organization.

This book, therefore, is designed to assist practicing school principals, as well as those who are newly appointed, in reviewing the central issues and in making appropriate decisions for a variety of situations that tend to occur in the administration of a school building.

Each chapter describes a variety of real situations that are certain to reoccur during the course of any principal's career. These illustrations involve the central office administration, Boards of Education, assistant principals, department chairpersons, supervisors, superintendents and assistant superintendents of schools, parents and parent groups, students and teachers—all from the perspective of the building principal.

Various techniques are used to simulate reality. Case studies, newspaper articles, meetings, telephone calls, office confrontations, faculty sessions, role-playing, short stories and in-service group discussions are designed to provide insights into central issues and solutions to key problems in the daily experiences of school administrators.

After the reader forms an opinion or discusses the Key Issues listed for each situation with other administrators, Analysis and Guidelines sections should be read. These sections set forth courses of action leading to the successful resolution of typical problems as confronted and solved previously by experienced, competent principals. The situations described have been selected carefully to represent the many problem areas building administrators are likely to encounter.

In that regard, the text is divided into the organizational and "people" problem areas of any school system. The focused situations described, which most school principals have faced at one time or another, include the following:

Central Office
- The newly hired superintendent is determined to "shake things up."
- The central office and the principal relinquish authority to a status teacher who abuses that power.
- The central office supervisor is willing to "go to war" to initiate an unwanted change in your building.
- The building principal knows when and how to obtain outside professional assistance.
- The principal demonstrates how to work with the assistant superintendent for instruction to implement a mandated program.

The Board of Education
- Analyze situations that require general Board of Education policy decisions.
- Deal effectively with Board of Education members who attempt to assume administrative responsibilities in your building.
- Prevent inappropriate negotiation activity by misguided Board members.
- Organize positive visits of Board members to your building.
- Involve the Board of Education in situations involving other education agencies.

The Community
- Parental objection can change decisions.
- A parent lobby can exert political pressure to force a program into the schools.
- A parent's input may provide valuable insights into teacher-student relationships.
- A PTA can become a true partner in educational improvement.
- A taxpayer can brew trouble at the supermarket.

The Assistant Principal
- The building administrator mends the links in a broken chain of command.
- The principal is required to evaluate one of his supervisors.

A WORD FROM THE AUTHORS 11

- The assistant principal tackles in-school desegregation problems with the support of the principal.
- Students and teachers can aid in solving problems that concern them.
- The assistant principal is given responsibility for seeking outside funding sources.

Students

- What should a principal do when students protest policy or procedure?
- What should a principal do when students or parents go straight to the superintendent or Board of Education?
- What should the principal do with the rebellious student who manufactures his or her own cause?
- What should the principal do about a disputed grade?
- What should the building administrator do for a student who has dropped out—in his seat?

Teachers

- The Guidance Department and the principal challenge a veteran staff to retain marginal students.
- The Union challenges the right of the principal to evaluate teachers.
- The building administrator tries to prevent and overcome teacher burnout.
- The principal moves quickly to salvage a potentially fine new teacher who is off to a poor start.
- The principal works informally with veteran master teachers to promote a better school.

The Change Process

- A principal who leads must not lose his or her ability to order change in negative situations.
- A principal must have an open door—that she or he closes from time to time to get work done.
- A leader can lead best by knowing how and when to establish a team at the top.

- A building administrator must know when to visit classrooms, halls and other school areas—and what to do after weighing feedback and his or her own observations.
- A building administrator can sense the fourth dimension of administration—timing.

Curriculum Leadership

- How does a principal retrain a veteran faculty as mandated by the State Department of Education?
- How does a principal determine areas of needed curriculum improvement and involve the faculty?
- How does a principal channel student energy into constructive co-curricular activities?
- How does a principal deal with telephone campaigns aimed at changing the school curriculum?
- How does a principal initiate renewal and positive attitudes among the entire faculty?

This text, then, was written as a useful desk reference for practicing school administrators, as an in-service aid in staff development work with interns and newly appointed principals, and as an instrument to initiate discussions at meetings and to evaluate patterns of action on similar situations and problems.

Kenneth Dunn
and
Rita Dunn

Contents

A Word from the Authors ... 9

Chapter 1
Functioning Effectively with the Central Office—17

SITUATION 1	Dealing with the "New Broom" Superintendent Virginia L. Kavanagh	18
SITUATION 2	Overcoming the Domineering Ombudsman Carole A. Decker	23
SITUATION 3	Initiating a Mandated Program with a Partially Reluctant Staff Gene Geisert	27
SITUATION 4	Using Professional Consultants Richard Sinatra	31
SITUATION 5	Setting Goals with District Administrators Rita Dunn and Kenneth Dunn	37

Chapter 2
Working with Boards of Education—45

SITUATION 6	Reaching Goals for Students Through Policy Decisions Barbara Shay	46
SITUATION 7	Coping with Board Members Who Try to Administer a Principal's Building John Spiridakis	49
SITUATION 8	Dealing with Divided or Misguided Board Members Gene Geisert	52

SITUATION 9	Planning for Board of Education Visits to Your Building Rita Dunn and Kenneth Dunn	55
SITUATION 10	Bridging Relationships Between Schools and Other Educational Units Barbara Shay	61

Chapter 3
Enlisting Community Cooperation—65

SITUATION 11	Responding to Parental Pressure Donal F. Buckley	66
SITUATION 12	Establishing Curriculum Advisory Groups Richard Sinatra	69
SITUATION 13	Dealing with Written Complaints Zarif Bacilious	74
SITUATION 14	Making the PTA a Partner Angela Bruno	78
SITUATION 15	Overcoming Supermarket Griping and Sniping at a New Program James R. Campbell and John Swanchak	81

Chapter 4
Supervising Assistant Principals—91

SITUATION 16	Linking the Chain of Command Within a Building Virginia L. Kavanagh	92
SITUATION 17	Evaluating the Instructional Effectiveness of the Assistant Principal Rita Dunn and Kenneth Dunn	97
SITUATION 18	Working on Desegregation Problems Shirley A. Griggs	108
SITUATION 19	Listening to Students with a Fair, Consistent Ear Carole A. Decker	113

CONTENTS

SITUATION 20	Delegating Higher Order Tasks—Sources of Outside Funding Shirley A. Griggs	117

Chapter 5
Improving Student School Participation—125

SITUATION 21	Reacting to Student Protest John Swanchak and James R. Campbell	126
SITUATION 22	Bypassing the Chain of Command John Swanchak and James R. Campbell	131
SITUATION 23	Dealing with the Rebel Without a Cause John Swanchak and James R. Campbell	137
SITUATION 24	Handling the Disputed Grade William McLaughlin	144
SITUATION 25	Helping the Student Who Fails to Pass Competency Exams John Swanchak and James R. Campbell	148

Chapter 6
Motivating the Teaching Staff—153

SITUATION 26	Stimulating a Veteran Faculty to Reach Marginal Students Shirley A. Griggs	154
SITUATION 27	Overcoming Union Manipulation and Pressures Gene Geisert	160
SITUATION 28	Preventing and Overcoming Burnout William Sanders	163
SITUATION 29	Improving an Individual Teacher's Performance Jean Hazelton	167
SITUATION 30	Dealing with Low Teacher Morale Joseph M. Aquino and Erika Wick	171

Chapter 7
Managing the Change Process—175

SITUATION 31	Upholding Students' Rights and Eliminating Questionable Practices Patricia A. Green	176
SITUATION 32	Planning Time and Priorities: How to Close an Always Open Door Erika Wick and Joseph M. Aquino	180
SITUATION 33	Using Regional Accreditation to Design Teams at the Top Shirley A. Griggs	185
SITUATION 34	Visiting Classrooms Is Only Part of Supervision Kathy Shanahan	190
SITUATION 35	Making the Right Supervisory Decision at the Right Time Donal F. Buckley	194

Chapter 8
Leading Staff and Community in Instructional Improvement—199

SITUATION 36	Reviewing and Improving the Curriculum Josephine Gemake	200
SITUATION 37	Retraining Faculty Josephine Gemake	205
SITUATION 38	Involving Students in Cocurricular Activities Shirley A. Griggs	209
SITUATION 39	Obtaining Public Input and Acceptance Shirley A. Griggs	213
SITUATION 40	Exhibiting Leadership Qualities Kathy Shanahan	216

Index   221

1
Functioning Effectively with the Central Office

SITUATION 1

> PROBLEM: Dealing with the "New Broom" Superintendent
>
> SITUATION: Bowling Alley Gossip

by
Virginia L. Kavanagh

The scene takes place in a bowling alley in the town of Linville, a metropolitan suburb. The cast of characters includes teachers and administrators in a school district of approximately six hundred educational personnel. They are gathered here as part of the district's bowling league. It is October, six weeks into the school term, and the subject of the comments is the new superintendent who was appointed in August. Dr. Dempster is forty-two years old, bright, attractive, and assertive.

"How do you like that guy? Did you see his latest memo? The man must have nothing better to do than sit and use paper!"

"What memo?"

"Oh, the one on 'Professional Commitment.' Didn't you get that one yet?"

"No. What's it all about?"

"You'll probably get it Monday. It just arrived this afternoon. He wants to come and meet the staff of each of the buildings. He wants to get to know the teachers and talk with them about professional commitment."

"Professional commitment? What do you think he means?"

"You know what he means. He wants us to give up additional hours to develop curriculum, to meet with parents in the community, to stay after school and run all kinds of activities, attend workshops on our own time and really prove that we are dedicated. What he really wants us to do is work fifteen extra hours a week for no additional pay."

"Listen, is it true what I heard about Dempster? The guy is just here as a 'hatchet man,' brought in to do the Board's dirty work, chop heads, get rid of people?"

"Sure, it's true. Didn't you hear what he pulled in the last place he was?"

"No, what's that?"

"Well, under the guise, of course, of reorganizing the Junior and Senior High for efficiency's sake, he had the Junior and Senior High merged into one administrative structure. That means they got rid of the Junior High principal, and they no longer needed Junior High chairpersons, either. They simply had one person for each subject area called a 'coordinator'—without tenure and with less pay."

"You're kidding."

"I wish I were."

"Hey, what is it with this character, Dempster? I mean the way I hear it they have three new people up in the District Office, all flunkies he brought in with him."

"Oh, sure. The man told the Board that they didn't really need all those expensive people they had there. They didn't need an assistant superintendent for curriculum and so forth. So, that's all being looked at, and they think it's going to be reorganized, and all of a sudden we're going to have 'directors of.' Somebody else said it's going to be 'administrative assistant to.' No assistant superintendents so they won't have to pay as much, and they won't have any authority. They'll just report to him."

"What are they going to do with the people who are in the administration now?"

"Well, since they're abolishing their jobs, they might give them an opportunity to apply for these new positions with less money and very little power. Otherwise, his flunkies will take over those positions."

"What's with Dempster?"

"What's with him? The man is forty-two years old. He was a young superintendent. I heard he was a superintendent at thirty-four, and this is his third superintendency. I can understand why. They probably had to bounce him out of the other two places. He'd do anything to convince the Board he was saving them money. He couldn't care less about the rest of us. I just hope it doesn't take us four years to get rid of him!"

KEY ISSUES

A. How can the principal help the staff sift fact from rumor?
B. How can the principal apprise the new superintendent of his staff's strengths and special qualifications?
C. How can the principal objectively evaluate the merits of new procedures that may be instituted?
D. How can the principal make a good case for his present programs without appearing to be self-serving?
E. How can the principal allay staff fears and resentments?
F. How can the principal moderate the superintendent's behavior if, in fact, it seems precipitous and without merit?
G. How does the principal learn to deal with this seeming "new broom" superintendent without feeling threatened?
H. What can the principal do to generate a mutual respect on the part of staff and superintendent for each other?
I. How can the principal become involved in the decisions of central office organization that affect him and his staff?

ANALYSIS

Apparently, Dr. Dempster has come to Linville with a predetermined, negative reputation. The wise principal would like to sift opinion from fact. The traditional avenue open to him is the word-of-mouth of colleagues who may have worked in Dr. Dempster's previous districts. However, the principal would have to discern how much of what was being reported was objective and how much was colored by the individual who served as reporter. Perhaps the wisest course of action might be to disregard the reputation and begin to deal with the reality. That is, the principal should not prejudge motives or behavior and should deal, instead, with Dr. Dempster as he currently performs.

For instance, the principal ought not to interpret a memo that calls for a meeting with the staff to discuss "professional commitment" and assume that means asking for extra, unpaid time on the part of the staff. The superintendent should be permitted to address the group and to clarify his intentions precisely. Furthermore, the prinicpal should not assume that when a memo entitled "Organizational Structure" is received, it automatically suggests that restructuring is preordained or that, per se, it is negative. Therefore, since the principal really has no other accurate way of separating the facts from the rumors, he must deal only with either what is presented to him or with what actually occurs.

However, the principal should be sufficiently realistic to understand that what he overheard in that bowling alley was a growing paranoia on the part of the staff and other administrators—a concern that should be addressed. Most persons are uncertain when a new leader appears on the scene. "How will I be received? Will my work be appreciated? Will my contributions be valued?" Because of such attitudes, one of the principal's first tasks should be to make his staff and their unique qualifications and strengths known to the superintendent.

This can be accomplished either informally during a meeting, or it can be done formally by forwarding some biographical data or resumés that would include the kinds of activities in which the staff has been involved. A further way to allay fear is to have the staff and superintendent meet each other. Permit the superintendent the opportunity to outline his plans and aspirations, thereby providing the faculty with an opportunity to make evaulations based upon his presentation rather than hearsay. Such meetings could offer opportunities for direct principal and staff involvement in future planning and decisions.

Another approach that the principal should initiate is the objective review of his programs and procedures. Have he and the staff been operating with a well-conceived plan? If they have achieved a measure of success, the principal should be prepared to share such programs with the superintendent. It is only fair to assume that the new administrator might have alternate perceptions that conceivably could enhance programs, or that he might propose procedures that could improve them further. One way for the principal to avoid feeling threatened is to maintain an open mind; he could discuss the situation objectively with his staff and be prepared to make needed changes. If, indeed, his objective is to conduct a high-quality program, he should be willing to discuss, consider and/or accept alternative viewpoints. He also might be able to teach the "New Broom" that some things are excellent exactly as they are!

In the matter of human relationships, if the new superintendent appears to be immoderate in the kinds and scope of changes that he proposes, the principal should have the courage to discuss with him approaches to faculty acceptance that may be necessary for success. Rather than assume an all-knowing stance, he would do well to indicate that he merely is willing to share his previous experience with the persons involved.

Ultimately, an overriding problem that the principal faces is how to generate a mutual respect between staff and superintendent. The principal should be thoughtful and considerate of other positions. His objective should be to help others develop an understanding of the concerns and pressures of their experiences—including limitations on time and resources. He needs to promote reciprocal responses to the question, "What can we do to make the process of education most beneficial to students and faculty?" The fact that both groups (administration and staff) must have input into the solution should be maintained as the operant principle.

GUIDELINES

1. Listen to all rumors and hearsay—then disclaim all that is not true with facts and reasons through every formal and informal channel at your disposal.
2. Bring the facts about your faculty and programs to the new chief executive (or other new central office personnel) through direct meetings and written reports.
3. Suggest ways in which to become involved directly in planning and deciding changes and programs that affect your students, your faculty and the administration of your building. These may include, but are not limited to:
   - an administrative council consisting of superintendent, key central office personnel and principals;
   - a sounding board committee of administrators and teachers representing all levels;
   - an informal caucus of administrators and superintendent every month, and/or
   - a district-wide committee of teachers, principals and central office administrators to discuss key program goals such as writing skills, reporting to parents, leisure reading, mathematics skills, programs for the talented and gifted, and so on.

SITUATION 2

> **PROBLEM:** Overcoming the Domineering Ombudsman
>
> **SITUATION:** Conversation Between Teacher and Student

by
Carole A. Decker

The young man was visibly upset as he walked along the school hallway.

"What's the matter?" asked Ms. Kent.

"Oh, nothin'," said the student.

"You sure look 'down in the mouth,'" the teacher replied.

"Well, I'm just not feeling so great today. I've got a big problem."

"Do you want to tell me about it?"

"No, I'll be all right," David muttered.

"OK," she said, "but if you need someone to talk to, you know I'll listen."

"Thanks," said David, sounding desolate.

Several days later, David, finishing his junior year at Oceanville High School, lingered in Ms. Kent's room after class, and asked if she was free. The English teacher put aside the work she had been doing and invited the student to sit down.

"I've got a decision to make," David announced, "and I'm not sure what to do."

"Tell me about it," Ms. Kent said, "and we'll see if I can help."

"Well, my parents want me to go to one of the military academies, and Mr. Scion, the ombudsman, is pressuring me, too."

"Do you want to go?" asked Ms. Kent.

"I'm not sure," said David. "I don't want to hurt my parents' feelings, and I know it would make it easier for them not to have to pay tuition. But, you always told me I could be a writer if I really applied myself."

"Yes, that's true. You have talent. I believe you could be a writer if you tried."

"I really think that's what I'd like to do, and I don't see how a military academy would allow me that freedom, or even help me to learn the skills of writing." David was relaxing and making Ms. Kent his confidante.

"I'd rather doubt that it would," Ms. Kent replied.

"Mr. Scion guarantees that he'll get me into Annapolis. He says my grades are good enough; and with the grade he'll give me in his Senior English class, it'll be a snap to be accepted."

"That sounds wonderful," said the teacher.

"And," continued David, "I'm into lots of extracurricular activities, and he'll use that to make my chances even better."

"With your background you can get into any university you choose," stated Ms. Kent.

"Yes, but Mr. Scion won't help me if I take your Advanced Placement English next year. I know it'll be more interesting, but my parents insist that I take Mr. Scion's English course so he'll help me get an appointment. I know I won't learn much. He just wants to sign up a big class." David was dejected.

"Well, why don't you take my Advanced Placement English anyway? It's a better choice for your elective. Even the Naval Academy would prefer it to regular Senior English," said the teacher.

"Because," said David flatly, "Mr. Scion is the only one who can get me into a service academy; he as much as told me so. All the kids know his rule. If you want his help, you have to take his course."

"Yes, so I've heard." Ms. Kent was reluctant to make the comment, but felt compelled to help the young man. "Let's ask Mr. Ford (the principal) what he thinks. Maybe we can solve your problem without hurting your chances with either Annapolis or any other college. I think you need more time to decide where you want to go, and taking AP English will be useful no matter which college you choose. Let's see Mr. Ford tomorrow."

"Thanks," smiled David weakly. "I feel better. I'll talk to my parents tonight."

That same afternoon, Ms. Kent spoke with the principal and outlined David's dilemma; she asked how the school might best help. Mr. Ford, tersely and brusquely, told her to "mind her own business," and to stay out of the matter completely. Ms. Kent pressed the issue; she was told that as school "ombudsman," Mr. Scion had been empowered by the central office to devote most of his time to helping students gain admission to colleges and that his record of success, particularly with the service academies, made him eminently more knowledgeable than she. She was dismissed from the principal's office as if she were a disciplined student.

Bristling at being given such short shrift, the spunky English teacher quietly researched the background of the situation. What she discovered appalled her; "ombudsman" was nothing but a self-designated title. Mr. Scion had seen a need for effective career guidance some years ago, and he had undertaken to fill that need. The faculty, the principal, the Guidance Department and a timid central office administration simply had accepted an escalated, originally voluntary act as a fait accompli. Now, through a steady accretion of responsibility, Mr. Scion had become the high school's alternative (and most powerful) guidance counselor. Students were, in fact, taking his one English course in order to ingratiate themselves and gain his support for their college aspirations. They were trading their senior year academic freedom for his assistance. He, in turn, was utilizing their immaturity for his self-enhancement. The school's administrators, though aware of his gambit, permitted its continuation by pretending that the greater good was being served.

KEY ISSUES

A. Central to this situation is the manner in which the district's and the school's administrative authority is exercised or abdicated; how students can become pawns in a political chess game.

B. The central office and the high school principal should have promulgated guidelines for the ombudsman position, its responsibilities and how its representative would function within the school.

C. One teacher should not be permitted such power over course options and college choices. Students ought not to feel that they must take a particular teacher's class in order to enhance their chances of obtaining the necessary assistance in gaining admittance into an academy, a college or a university.

D. All college-bound students should have equal access to

college entrance assistance without having to please an ombudsman or *any* teacher. They should not feel compelled to take unwanted elective courses.
E. A high school principal should not be so rigid as to mandate that student assistance and guidance may derive only from designated personnel. Most students prefer to seek counseling and advice from adults with whom they have rapport.

ANALYSIS

David did very well academically during his junior year. He enrolled in Mr. Scion's Senior English course in his senior year and received a grade of "A." He was accepted into the Naval Academy with Mr. Scion's recommendation. In October of his sophomore year at Annapolis his grades slipped drastically, and he dropped out. He was last reported working as a stock boy at a local supermarket.

Ms. Kent, furious at this waste, was determined to do something about the failure of the school. She enlisted the help of the other teachers in the English Department. They, too, were aware of the problem and agreed to support her protest. They petitioned the principal, and, as a group, expressed their views with the ombudsman present at the meeting.

Mr. Scion, insulted and adamant, shouted that only he knew "how to get these kids into service academies"; he cursed them all and stomped from the room. The principal shrugged and said that Mr. Scion did do his work well and that he was not going to withdraw support of these efforts. Case closed! The other teachers left Mr. Ford's office angry and frustrated.

Another school year passed during which Mr. Scion shunned those who had opposed him. He continued to exert his influence over college-bound students while the other teachers' efforts to aid those youngsters were frustrated and subverted. Mr. Ford then retired as building principal, and the new principal was asked to confront the problem.

GUIDELINES

1. Principals should establish a collegial relationship with the school's teaching faculty to make the education of their charges as successful as possible.

LY WITH THE CENTRAL OFFICE

d receive rational, insightful and person-
ig and guidance concerning the courses they

udsman, if it is to be established, should
ned responsibilities.

lors, chairpersons, ombudsman—all staff
d focus on the needs of each student. Self-
lvancement develop most easily from a
ional giving.

s responsibility to be certain that adopted
e followed by all staff members.

SITUATION 3

PROBLEM: Initiating a Mandated Program with a Partially Reluctant Staff

SITUATION: Interoffice Memorandum

by
Gene Geisert

TO: Betty Hill, Assistant Superintendent for Instruction
FROM: Mike Keen, Superintendent
SUBJECT: Complaints Concerning Phase-in of Mastery Learning Program

Three different Board members mentioned that they received telephone calls from parents complaining about the proposed phase-in of the Mastery Learning Program we re-

> cently adopted as the result of a Board policy decision to use that process to respond to the differing academic levels and styles of our student population.
>
> The calls appear to have been stimulated by some of our veteran teachers at the high school. Please look into the matter and take appropriate steps to allay their fears and gain their support.

Betty Hill reached for the phone and used the direct line to Herb Starr, the high school principal. Herb, ever on top of things, already knew and had tried to reach her earlier. He agreed to come to her office right after dismissal time.

Betty and Herb carefully reviewed the change strategy that had been developed to insure an effective implementation of the Mastery Learning Program. The program was to be the cornerstone of the district plan to improve student achievement and success. These were critical factors in the attempt to regain community support for budget approvals, badly needed support staff and building rehabilitation.

Betty instinctively knew that the superintendent's job would be very much "on the line" pending an assessment of the Mastery Learning Program's eventual impact on achievement scores. She was supportive of the program, and she certainly wanted to protect Dr. Keen's position in the district. Herb was an advocate of both, too; in addition, he had four years until retirement and wanted to reverse what seemed to him to be a softening in standards at the High School.

During the initial teacher workshops, Betty had observed a clique of veteran teachers who seemed rather hostile toward the consultants; at the time she had considered their remarks as being representative of resentment toward an outsider who had chided them on the comparative lack of learner success in the district. Herb remembered the group and noted that he could list each of their names. He admitted that he hadn't been very concerned about their reactions at those first few sessions; he certainly thought they'd give the program a fair change. Now, however, it was possible that a concerted effort to discredit the program was at the center of those teachers' hostile behavior.

On reflection, Betty also considered that another part of their hidden agenda might be to cause the program to fail and ultimately to embarrass (and thus get rid of) the young superintendent who

FUNCTIONING EFFECTIVELY WITH THE CENTRAL OFFICE

was hired specifically to shake up the district and to reverse the downhill academic trend that appeared to be developing into a pattern.

Herb concurred and reported that the same group had been urging him to "take it easy and enjoy the last few years before retirement." "After all," they'd rejoined, "we built this school's reputation, and we're entitled to some peace and stability; and so are you, Herb!" His appeals to their professionalism and the needs of the students were rejected. "Who's gonna appreciate all that effort?" they retorted.

KEY ISSUES

A. Can a principal persuade recalcitrant veteran teachers about the wisdom of anything new if there is a predisposition toward rejection of anything other than the status quo?

B. What strategies can be employed to initiate promising programs, mandated or otherwise, despite partial or substantive opposition?

C. How can the principal gain the support and assistance of the central office for programs of mutual concern?

ANALYSIS AND ACTION

Betty and Herb agreed on a strategy, and Betty dictated a confidential memo to the superintendent outlining their approach.

CONFIDENTIAL MEMORANDUM

TO: Dr. Michael Keen
FROM: Betty Hill and Herb Starr
SUBJECT: Phase-in of Mastery Learning Program

Herb Starr and I both agree that the most critical technical requirement for installing a district-wide Mastery Learning Program is that every teacher be qualified and committed to this approach, particularly at the high school where the largest pocket of resistance appears to exist.

When such a commitment is lacking, disapproving teachers will tend not to use the new professional practices required for the successful implementation of the adopted concept.

> In our estimation, approximately one-third of our teaching staff at the high school is eagerly awaiting the implementation of the Mastery approach. Another third is believed to have adopted a cautious "wait and see" attitude; the final third (which in our district for various reasons, tends to be veteran teachers) adamantly opposes the move. The overall percentage appears to be much more favorable toward the change at our junior high and elementary schools.
>
> In view of the above, Herb and I suggest that you consider a gradual phase-in of the program, selecting only the most interested and committed teachers for the first stages. The consultants have agreed to concentrate their efforts and provide the Phase I teachers with thorough and intensified training which would enable them to learn, apply and share with others the new learner-centered practices.
>
> These "key" teachers would be most likely to ensure the successful implementation of the program. Once this approach achieves success (i.e., achievement scores significantly improve next year), the second group of teachers could be brought on board. We believe that by the third year it will be very difficult for any teachers to fight the successes we anticipate.
>
> Herb also wants to assure you that some veteran teachers are in the positively disposed group.
>
> While I realize that our recommendation requires a three-year time frame, I believe it represents the best course of action to break down the present negative buildup and still permit us to move forward with a good chance of eliciting widespread faculty support.

The superintendent accepted the two administrators' strategy and rejected negotiation, strong memos, team meetings and various other approaches; he believed that their careful assessment of the situation and suggested course of action had the best chance for success.

In any new program there are unavoidable problems with implementation procedures and unplanned delays that frustrate both teachers and administrators. Each provocation would reawaken criticisms from teachers who still prefer to do things their way.

The administration decided to take the time needed and to encourage the strongest teacher/principal teams at both the high school and other buildings to begin the new process in ways that would promote success.

GUIDELINES

1. Listen very carefully to all faculty members as they react to changes or new programs. Assess attitudes, but do not spend time on motives; actions or behaviors are what are central to the success of any change.
2. Work closely and candidly with the central office personnel given responsibility for programs, projects and changes.
3. Consider options that will guarantee success. Involve able, motivated staff who are determined to make a project work.
4. Use the variables of time, location, personnel and support from the central office wisely to initiate and sustain new programs.

SITUATION 4

> PROBLEM: Using Professional Consultants
>
> SITUATION: Responding to Direction from the Central Office

by
Richard Sinatra

The superintendent directed the principal of the Springfield Elementary School to redesign the reading program in an effort to raise state basic skills test scores. The school had been focusing on a basal reading series and "ability" reading groups—a traditional approach that had served its pupils well for many years but that no longer obtained the same high scores.

Jim Renzo, the principal, knew that the student body had changed; basic intelligence was lower and interest in academics seemed to have declined. He knew that two professors at a local university had been working on an instrument that determines what occurs during the time span when reading is taught. The next morning Jim called Bob Roberts, one of the researchers, for an appointment. During their meeting that week, Roberts explained that a great deal of time, energy and often heated argument in a school is spent on comparing the merits of one curriculum program against another—even though the rationale and procedures of each approach might be similar. Instead of making program judgments and initiating curriculum changes based on minor distinctions between product format and content, administrators should look at what occurs during the teaching of content. After all, with reading in particular, researchers have provided conflicting data. Some report that it is the *teacher* and not the method that makes the difference (Artley, 1972); or that it is the faculty, *under the leadership of the principal*, systematically using a system in which they have become competent and in which they have confidence, that makes a difference in a school's achievement (Singer, 1977); or that the correct matching of a complementary approach and the student's perceptual strengths produces increased reading achievement (Urbschat, 1977; Carbo, 1980; and Wheeler, 1980); or that students who are taught through their individual learning styles evidence statistically significant increased reading speed and comprehension scores (Pizzo, 1981; Krimsky, 1982).

Roberts went on: "Investigations conducted during the mid-70s, seeking answers to the question of which instructional variables most influenced student achievement, revealed some startling findings that are highly important for principals and curriculum supervisors to consider. First, a positive relationship exists between instructional time allocated to a curriculum area and student achievement (Fisher, et.al., 1976). Teachers control and allocate their own time in the teaching process and direct students in ways which strongly influence and condition the kinds and degrees of their active learning. However, when allocated time was compared against 'engaged' student time (the actual amount of time in which youngsters really concentrate on the task) in reading and mathematics, it was found that many second graders were engaged in reading activities only about fifty percent of the time allocated to reading (Fisher, et.al., 1976), and fifty percent of the time allocated to math (Filby, 1977)."

Moreover, Filby reported that sustained reading time was remarkably low in some classes, with as little as 15 minutes per day actually devoted to reading. In another report by Fisher, et.al. (1978), it was noted that the average engagement rate for second and fifth graders in reading and math was between 70 and 75 percent. However, those authors believed that the higher engagement rate occurred because they did not exclude "transition activities" such as student movement and waiting time from the allocated reading and math time as was done in other studies.

Recently, Stallings (1980) reported, after observing 87 secondary school remedial reading classes, that it is not only a question of how much time is allocated, but also how that time is used. "Interactive verbal activities like reading aloud and class discussion, along with positive, corrective feedback, were highly related to the success of less able students."

"You see, Jim," Roberts continued, "these findings were based on very detailed observations of teachers and students during instruction over a period of time. By synthesizing many of the observational procedures used in several studies, I am now able to provide principals and curriculum supervisors a means of objectively quantifying how teachers and students spend their time during reading instruction."

KEY ISSUES

A. Should curriculum or program change be attempted by staff and principal without outside assistance?
B. If outside assistance is sought, how should it be selected?
C. Who should be involved from *within* the school?
D. What should the principal do to ensure pilot program success?
E. Where contradictory research exists, shouldn't the principal seek alternative sources and reports?

ANALYSIS AND SOLUTIONS

Jim liked what Roberts had to say; he was impressed with the way the researcher blended data and the practical aspects of day-today teaching. Roberts outlined an approach for beginning a pilot program to assess what was actually happening when reading was taught in Jim's building. Jim advised that he would form a faculty group to consider the venture and would get back to Roberts in a couple of weeks.

Teachers at each grade level were invited to form a committee to consider the superintendent's directive and Roberts' proposal to implement a pilot program to assess what was actually occurring during the periods allocated to reading. Jay Perrin, a primary teacher, looked puzzled. "I don't see the direct relationship between the need for a redesigned reading program and monitoring how the time is being spent on reading when it is being taught," she posed. "There *is* a relationship between the two," countered Bee Gardiner, "but what is revealed will not necessarily indicate whether we ought to change our reading books and other resources, the amount of time we spend on reading, what we do during that time, and which kids need more or less time on the topic or different materials or methods. This is an unfocused approach; or, rather, it is focused in a direction different from what I would have considered!" The sixth grade teacher continued. "Frankly, I took a course with Roberts while I was getting my master's degree, and although he quotes research, I always kind of felt he was a bit off target. He *sounds* practical, but he's somewhere up in space!"

Jim was taken aback. Had Roberts misdirected his attention? He asked the other members of the group for their opinions.

Jay Perrin suggested that Jim tell Roberts that the committee had decided to investigate other possibilities before making a commitment to the pilot program as described by the researcher. She then added that it might be advantageous for each committee member to assume the responsibility for looking up the studies that Roberts had mentioned, just to get a feeling for the topic. She also remembered a Professor Carbo who had impressed her when she spoke at the National Association for Supervision and Curriculum Development Annual Conference the previous year. Carbo had advocated "matching reading approaches to students' perceptual strengths."

Jim remembered Roberts talking about Carbo's work and thought it *would* be a good idea to pursue that particular line.

A fourth grade teacher had heard about Lynch's study on time of day and volunteered to follow through on that at the local library. Another person said he'd call the major book publishers and share their concerns about the need for a new program, requesting that either copies of new offerings be forwarded to the school for examination and/or that a representative be sent to discuss the matter.

Patty Bren said that she'd contact the International Reading Association president and request guidelines for the adoption of new texts, and at the same time, Helena Hode exploded with, "Maybe we shouldn't consider a *text* or *series* at all! I read an article that described a great New York City school that improved the reading levels of delinquent teenagers by using very high interest materials instead of books! Let me locate that publication, and I'll bring it in! Let's consider *really* good alternatives! Let's do it right if we're putting all this effort into it!"

GUIDELINES

1. Outside assistance is necessary if options are to be available and if newer concepts are to be considered.
2. Professionals within the school must be involved if on-target suggestions are to be incorporated successfully into any emerging program.
3. Involvement of staff often produces "ownership" of an idea or practice. It is wise to bring teachers into the discussion and planning at a beginning stage.
4. Consider many possible sources of information before adopting any new idea, practice, materials and so forth. Most people become involved in their own areas of concentration and often do not keep up with what is happening in other aspects of the field.
5. *Test* any program or materials that you are considering adopting with the actual children for whom they are intended. A pilot program is always a good idea before widespread adoption or purchase.
6. A central approach should be established for each pilot program. Experimental projects should focus on variables that can be monitored and evaluated; e.g., use of interest-based materials, diagnosis and prescription based on learning styles, learning to read through writing.

REFERENCES

A. S. Artley, "The Teacher Variable in the Teaching of Reading," in *The First R: Readings on Teaching Reading*, ed. by C. J. Wallen and S. Sebesta. Chicago, Illinois: Science Research Associates, Inc. (1972).

Marie Antonetti Carbo, "An Analysis of the Relationships Between the Modality Preferences of Kindergartners and Selected Reading Treatments As They Affect the Learning of a Basic Sight-Word Vocabulary," Ed.D. Dissertation, St. John's University (1980).

Nikola N. Filby, et al., *Allocated and Engaged Time in Different Content Areas of Second and Fifth Grade Reading and Mathematics Curriculum* (1977) : 29 (ED 137 315).

Charles W. Fisher, et al., *A Study of Instructional Time in Grade 2 Reading. Technical Report 11-4, BTES (Beginning Teacher Evaluation Study)* (1976) : 201 (ED 145 414).

Charles W. Fisher, et al., *Selected Findings from Phase III BTES. (Beginning Teacher Evaluation Study)* (1978) : 172 (ED 160 639).

Jeffrey Krimsky, "A Comparative Study of the Effects of Matching and Mismatching Fourth Grade Students With Their Learning Style Preference For the Environmental Element of Light and Their Subsequent Reading Speed and Accuracy Scores," Ed.D. Dissertation, St. John's University (1982).

Jeanne Pizzo, "An Investigation of the Relationships Between Selected Acoustic Environments and Sound, an Element of Learning Style, As They Affect Sixth Grade Students' Reading Achievement and Attitudes," Ed.D. Dissertation, St. John's University (1981).

Harry Singer, "Resolving Curricular Conflicts in the 1970's: Modifying the Hypothesis, It's the Teacher Who Makes the Difference in Reading Achivement." *Language Arts* 54 (February 1977) : 158-163.

Jane Stallings, "Allocated Academic Learning Time Revisited, or Beyond Time on Task," *Educational Researcher* 9 (December 1980) : 11-16.

Karen Spangenberg Urbschat, "A Study of Preferred Learning Modes and Their Relationship to the Amount of Recall of CVC Trigrams," Ph.D. Dissertation, Wayne State University (1977).

Roberta Wheeler, "An Alternative to Failure: Teaching Reading According to Students' Perceptual Strengths," *Kappa Delta Pi Record* 17, 2 (December, 1980) : 59-63.

SITUATION 5

> PROBLEM: Setting Goals with District Administrators
>
> SITUATION: The New Principal Arrives

by
Rita Dunn and Kenneth Dunn

Robert Wills, the newly appointed principal, and Mary Goodstein, the assistant superintendent for instruction, toured the building in early June. Bob wanted to see the students and teachers in action before he assumed the principalship officially on July 1.

He was aware that the previous principal, who had just left on a disability retirement, and the assistant superintendent were close friends. Mary Goodstein, however, was objective and supportive of instructional programs that met individual student needs. She wanted to view the school through Bob's eyes and then assess his goals for the building. After all, he had an unusually strong background in both primary and preschool education as a teacher, supervisor and college instructor.

The Richard K. Hart Early Childhood Center in Ivory Lane, Connecticut, was designed specifically to house an innovative primary school program. Its glass-enclosed dome and outer walls bordered on a tranquil suburban woodland that was picturesque and soothing. Its interior admitted natural daylight that brightened and cheered the huge, open-spaced learning environment from early morning to dusk.

The school population reflected an upper middle-class professional and business community that appreciated quality education and a program that enticed children into successful learning. Taxes were high, but the school district was supported loyally by its citizens who wanted educational excellence. The total annual per-pupil school expenditure was among the highest in the state, and because Richard K. Hart was a relatively new building, its appropriations included sufficient monies for extensive multimedia resources, instructional packages, supplies and technological equipment.

This Early Childhood Center housed 300 pupils and boasted a staff of 12 full-time teachers, one secretary, one principal, one principal's assistant, six paraprofessionals and two student teachers (every semester). Local parents had indicated an interest in assisting the teachers (many mothers were former teachers), but no training program had been formulated. Therefore, the principal had not utilized this volunteer service.

On this, his second visit, Bob was drawn immediately to the breathtaking panoramas visible through each glass wall. It was a lovely, warm, sun-drenched, day, but he noticed that no children were outdoors and no doors were open.

Children were clustered in various sections of the inner center areas. They were reading books, making charts, reading graphs, painting, playing with blocks and other games or just talking to each other or to one of the available adults. Around the outside walls of the Center were low bookcases, children's waist-high movable closets, boxes with materials that were still unpacked and cartons of pupil-made booklets, reports, dolls or creative arts.

At the middle of the Center was a series of round tables that had been established as instructional areas. These "learning stations" each held some math games, some blocks, a few brushes, two puppets, two basal readers entitled *Dick and Jane*, a microscope and some beads. No one was working at any of them. The game tables held blocks, paints, a few transparencies that appeared to be torn, a child's lost hat, and a huge fire engine. There were approximately 20 carpet squares under one of the game tables and many additional ones scattered about the Center.

The 300 children appeared to have been divided equally among the 12 professional teachers. Each group of pupils and a teacher had appropriated a part of the Center for themselves. The beautiful open-spaced feeling of the building appeared to be diminished by the clutter of children and resources. Wherever you walked, children were engaged either in silent reading (very young children for so many to be reading) or drawing, or were involved in independent quiet activity. The teachers, although they did interact with individual youngsters who sought their assistance, were engaged in examining materials from the partially opened supply cartons and were giving instructions to the student teachers who were trying to become familiar with the curriculum by reading the teachers' lesson plan books. Aides were running off dittos and writing children's names on workbooks, crayon boxes and other materials.

The principal's assistant, Mrs. James, extended an extremely cordial welcome to Bob and the assistant superintendent. She graciously guided them through the Early Childhood Center, emphasizing the many independent activities in which the youngsters were engaged. She laughingly said that these pupils were so bright and so mature that they "…really don't need direction from anyone! They could work all day completely absorbed in their own interests!"

Teachers, too, were friendly and hospitable. They eagerly pointed out the learning stations, the game tables and the multitude of media that were available. They admitted that much of it still was unpacked, but added that they really had to learn to use it themselves before they could permit the children to do so. They left their plan books in a conspicuous place on their desks so that the principal could see how detailed and well-prepared they were. In actuality, a few teachers' plans reflected schedules two and three weeks in advance.

When questioned about the program, teachers quickly responded that this was "an open classroom modeled after the British Primary School." They explained that children selected their own resources, planned their own activities and engaged in them for as long as their interests were maintained. They added that this was "an integrated day approach."

Bob looked around the Center. The children did seem absorbed. There were few incidents of boisterous conduct or conflict. Children everywhere were working quietly, appeared to be self-directed and occasionally intereacted with the adults in the area. When a child did solicit counseling, the adults were responsive and warm, and responded to the child's question with short, simple statements. Some children wandered around and talked to each other and did not seem to mind the cluttered environment. If there was interaction with the available resources, the child who selected the materials used them until he was finished, at which point another child might use them where they were left.

KEY ISSUES

A. What approach to assessment and goal-setting would work best in this situation?
B. How can the principal outline a program that will receive support from the Central Office and the staff?
C. What are the specific elements of an improvement program based on the stated current goals and an evaluation of how those goals are being met in the existing program? What needs to be changed in the goals of the Center and the teaching and learning strategies to meet them?

ANALYSIS

Mary Goodstein seemed uncomfortable as they sat at lunch after the three hours of observation.

Bob put her at ease. "I know what a great job Ann (the retired principal) did over the years for this district, and I know her illness kept her out of the building for a good part of this school year. There are many positive qualities in that building, and I hope you will aid me in making it even better."

The assistant superintendent was quite relieved. "It's obvious why we employed you, Bob, but we don't expect you to change things by next October. The parents have become more aware of the deficits of the program and really want to help."

"If there is any summer curriculum money in the budget, I'd like to meet with the teachers for a week if possible and then schedule meetings with parents in August. I will forward our observations and plans to you over the summer."

They shook hands warmly and left.

In August, Bob forwarded the following synthesized lists to Dr. Goodstein for comment and support in establishing workshops, parent sessions, the redesign of instructional areas and other items that required budgeting or Central Office approval.

A. Behaviors inappropriate to or absent from an effective instructional environment at our Early Childhood Center:

munity, to stay after school and run all kinds of activities, attend workshops on our own time and really prove that we are dedicated. What he really wants us to do is work fifteen extra hours a week for no additional pay."

"Listen, is it true what I heard about Dempster? The guy is just here as a 'hatchet man,' brought in to do the Board's dirty work, chop heads, get rid of people?"

"Sure, it's true. Didn't you hear what he pulled in the last place he was?"

"No, what's that?"

"Well, under the guise, of course, of reorganizing the Junior and Senior High for efficiency's sake, he had the Junior and Senior High merged into one administrative structure. That means they got rid of the Junior High principal, and they no longer needed Junior High chairpersons, either. They simply had one person for each subject area called a 'coordinator'—without tenure and with less pay."

"You're kidding."

"I wish I were."

"Hey, what is it with this character, Dempster? I mean the way I hear it they have three new people up in the District Office, all flunkies he brought in with him."

"Oh, sure. The man told the Board that they didn't really need all those expensive people they had there. They didn't need an assistant superintendent for curriculum and so forth. So, that's all being looked at, and they think it's going to be reorganized, and all of a sudden we're going to have 'directors of.' Somebody else said it's going to be 'administrative assistant to.' No assistant superintendents so they won't have to pay as much, and they won't have any authority. They'll just report to him."

"What are they going to do with the people who are in the administration now?"

"Well, since they're abolishing their jobs, they might give them an opportunity to apply for these new positions with less money and very little power. Otherwise, his flunkies will take over those positions."

"What's with Dempster?"

"What's with him? The man is forty-two years old. He was a young superintendent. I heard he was a superintendent at thirty-four, and this is his third superintendency. I can understand why. They probably had to bounce him out of the other two places. He'd do anything to convince the Board he was saving them money. He couldn't care less about the rest of us. I just hope it doesn't take us four years to get rid of him!"

KEY ISSUES

    A. How can the principal help the staff sift fact from rumor?
    B. How can the principal apprise the new superintendent of his staff's strengths and special qualifications?
    C. How can the principal objectively evaluate the merits of new procedures that may be instituted?
    D. How can the principal make a good case for his present programs without appearing to be self-serving?
    E. How can the principal allay staff fears and resentments?
    F. How can the principal moderate the superintendent's behavior if, in fact, it seems precipitous and without merit?
    G. How does the principal learn to deal with this seeming "new broom" superintendent without feeling threatened?
    H. What can the principal do to generate a mutual respect on the part of staff and superintendent for each other?
    I. How can the principal become involved in the decisions of central office organization that affect him and his staff?

ANALYSIS

Apparently, Dr. Dempster has come to Linville with a predetermined, negative reputation. The wise principal would like to sift opinion from fact. The traditional avenue open to him is the word-of-mouth of colleagues who may have worked in Dr. Dempster's previous districts. However, the principal would have to discern how much of what was being reported was objective and how much was colored by the individual who served as reporter. Perhaps the wisest course of action might be to disregard the reputation and begin to deal with the reality. That is, the principal should not prejudge motives or behavior and should deal, instead, with Dr. Dempster as he currently performs.

For instance, the principal ought not to interpret a memo that calls for a meeting with the staff to discuss "professional commitment" and assume that means asking for extra, unpaid time on the part of the staff. The superintendent should be permitted to address the group and to clarify his intentions precisely. Furthermore, the prinicipal should not assume that when a memo entitled "Organizational Structure" is received, it automatically suggests that restructuring is preordained or that, per se, it is negative. Therefore, since the principal really has no other accurate way of separating the facts from the rumors, he must deal only with either what is presented to him or with what actually occurs.

However, the principal should be sufficiently realistic to understand that what he overheard in that bowling alley was a growing paranoia on the part of the staff and other administrators—a concern that should be addressed. Most persons are uncertain when a new leader appears on the scene. "How will I be received? Will my work be appreciated? Will my contributions be valued?" Because of such attitudes, one of the principal's first tasks should be to make his staff and their unique qualifications and strengths known to the superintendent.

This can be accomplished either informally during a meeting, or it can be done formally by forwarding some biographical data or resumés that would include the kinds of activities in which the staff has been involved. A further way to allay fear is to have the staff and superintendent meet each other. Permit the superintendent the opportunity to outline his plans and aspirations, thereby providing the faculty with an opportunity to make evaulations based upon his presentation rather than hearsay. Such meetings could offer opportunities for direct principal and staff involvement in future planning and decisions.

Another approach that the principal should initiate is the objective review of his programs and procedures. Have he and the staff been operating with a well-conceived plan? If they have achieved a measure of success, the principal should be prepared to share such programs with the superintendent. It is only fair to assume that the new administrator might have alternate perceptions that conceivably could enhance programs, or that he might propose procedures that could improve them further. One way for the principal to avoid feeling threatened is to maintain an open mind; he could discuss the situation objectively with his staff and be prepared to make needed changes. If, indeed, his objective is to conduct a high-quality program, he should be willing to discuss, consider and/or accept alternative viewpoints. He also might be able to teach the "New Broom" that some things are excellent exactly as they are!

In the matter of human relationships, if the new superintendent appears to be immoderate in the kinds and scope of changes that he proposes, the principal should have the courage to discuss with him approaches to faculty acceptance that may be necessary for success. Rather than assume an all-knowing stance, he would do well to indicate that he merely is willing to share his previous experience with the persons involved.

Ultimately, an overriding problem that the principal faces is how to generate a mutual respect between staff and superintendent. The principal should be thoughtful and considerate of other positions. His objective should be to help others develop an understanding of the concerns and pressures of their experiences—including limitations on time and resources. He needs to promote reciprocal responses to the question, "What can we do to make the process of education most beneficial to students and faculty?" The fact that both groups (administration and staff) must have input into the solution should be maintained as the operant principle.

GUIDELINES

1. Listen to all rumors and hearsay—then disclaim all that is not true with facts and reasons through every formal and informal channel at your disposal.
2. Bring the facts about your faculty and programs to the new chief executive (or other new central office personnel) through direct meetings and written reports.
3. Suggest ways in which to become involved directly in planning and deciding changes and programs that affect your students, your faculty and the administration of your building. These may include, but are not limited to:
   - an administrative council consisting of superintendent, key central office personnel and principals;
   - a sounding board committee of administrators and teachers representing all levels;
   - an informal caucus of administrators and superintendent every month, and/or
   - a district-wide committee of teachers, principals and central office administrators to discuss key program goals such as writing skills, reporting to parents, leisure reading, mathematics skills, programs for the talented and gifted, and so on.

SITUATION 2

> PROBLEM: Overcoming the Domineering Ombudsman
>
> SITUATION: Conversation Between Teacher and Student

by
Carole A. Decker

The young man was visibly upset as he walked along the school hallway.

"What's the matter?" asked Ms. Kent.

"Oh, nothin'," said the student.

"You sure look 'down in the mouth,'" the teacher replied.

"Well, I'm just not feeling so great today. I've got a big problem."

"Do you want to tell me about it?"

"No, I'll be all right," David muttered.

"OK," she said, "but if you need someone to talk to, you know I'll listen."

"Thanks," said David, sounding desolate.

Several days later, David, finishing his junior year at Oceanville High School, lingered in Ms. Kent's room after class, and asked if she was free. The English teacher put aside the work she had been doing and invited the student to sit down.

"I've got a decision to make," David announced, "and I'm not sure what to do."

"Tell me about it," Ms. Kent said, "and we'll see if I can help."

"Well, my parents want me to go to one of the military academies, and Mr. Scion, the ombudsman, is pressuring me, too."

"Do you want to go?" asked Ms. Kent.

"I'm not sure," said David. "I don't want to hurt my parents' feelings, and I know it would make it easier for them not to have to pay tuition. But, you always told me I could be a writer if I really applied myself."

"Yes, that's true. You have talent. I believe you could be a writer if you tried."

"I really think that's what I'd like to do, and I don't see how a military academy would allow me that freedom, or even help me to learn the skills of writing." David was relaxing and making Ms. Kent his confidante.

"I'd rather doubt that it would," Ms. Kent replied.

"Mr. Scion guarantees that he'll get me into Annapolis. He says my grades are good enough; and with the grade he'll give me in his Senior English class, it'll be a snap to be accepted."

"That sounds wonderful," said the teacher.

"And," continued David, "I'm into lots of extracurricular activities, and he'll use that to make my chances even better."

"With your background you can get into any university you choose," stated Ms. Kent.

"Yes, but Mr. Scion won't help me if I take your Advanced Placement English next year. I know it'll be more interesting, but my parents insist that I take Mr. Scion's English course so he'll help me get an appointment. I know I won't learn much. He just wants to sign up a big class." David was dejected.

"Well, why don't you take my Advanced Placement English anyway? It's a better choice for your elective. Even the Naval Academy would prefer it to regular Senior English," said the teacher.

"Because," said David flatly, "Mr. Scion is the only one who can get me into a service academy; he as much as told me so. All the kids know his rule. If you want his help, you have to take his course."

"Yes, so I've heard." Ms. Kent was reluctant to make the comment, but felt compelled to help the young man. "Let's ask Mr. Ford (the principal) what he thinks. Maybe we can solve your problem without hurting your chances with either Annapolis or any other college. I think you need more time to decide where you want to go, and taking AP English will be useful no matter which college you choose. Let's see Mr. Ford tomorrow."

"Thanks," smiled David weakly. "I feel better. I'll talk to my parents tonight."

That same afternoon, Ms. Kent spoke with the principal and outlined David's dilemma; she asked how the school might best help. Mr. Ford, tersely and brusquely, told her to "mind her own business," and to stay out of the matter completely. Ms. Kent pressed the issue; she was told that as school "ombudsman," Mr. Scion had been empowered by the central office to devote most of his time to helping students gain admission to colleges and that his record of success, particularly with the service academies, made him eminently more knowledgeable than she. She was dismissed from the principal's office as if she were a disciplined student.

Bristling at being given such short shrift, the spunky English teacher quietly researched the background of the situation. What she discovered appalled her; "ombudsman" was nothing but a self-designated title. Mr. Scion had seen a need for effective career guidance some years ago, and he had undertaken to fill that need. The faculty, the principal, the Guidance Department and a timid central office administration simply had accepted an escalated, originally voluntary act as a fait accompli. Now, through a steady accretion of responsibility, Mr. Scion had become the high school's alternative (and most powerful) guidance counselor. Students were, in fact, taking his one English course in order to ingratiate themselves and gain his support for their college aspirations. They were trading their senior year academic freedom for his assistance. He, in turn, was utilizing their immaturity for his self-enhancement. The school's administrators, though aware of his gambit, permitted its continuation by pretending that the greater good was being served.

KEY ISSUES

A. Central to this situation is the manner in which the district's and the school's administrative authority is exercised or abdicated; how students can become pawns in a political chess game.

B. The central office and the high school principal should have promulgated guidelines for the ombudsman position, its responsibilities and how its representative would function within the school.

C. One teacher should not be permitted such power over course options and college choices. Students ought not to feel that they must take a particular teacher's class in order to enhance their chances of obtaining the necessary assistance in gaining admittance into an academy, a college or a university.

D. All college-bound students should have equal access to

college entrance assistance without having to please an ombudsman or *any* teacher. They should not feel compelled to take unwanted elective courses.

E. A high school principal should not be so rigid as to mandate that student assistance and guidance may derive only from designated personnel. Most students prefer to seek counseling and advice from adults with whom they have rapport.

ANALYSIS

David did very well academically during his junior year. He enrolled in Mr. Scion's Senior English course in his senior year and received a grade of "A." He was accepted into the Naval Academy with Mr. Scion's recommendation. In October of his sophomore year at Annapolis his grades slipped drastically, and he dropped out. He was last reported working as a stock boy at a local supermarket.

Ms. Kent, furious at this waste, was determined to do something about the failure of the school. She enlisted the help of the other teachers in the English Department. They, too, were aware of the problem and agreed to support her protest. They petitioned the principal, and, as a group, expressed their views with the ombudsman present at the meeting.

Mr. Scion, insulted and adamant, shouted that only he knew "how to get these kids into service academies"; he cursed them all and stomped from the room. The principal shrugged and said that Mr. Scion did do his work well and that he was not going to withdraw support of these efforts. Case closed! The other teachers left Mr. Ford's office angry and frustrated.

Another school year passed during which Mr. Scion shunned those who had opposed him. He continued to exert his influence over college-bound students while the other teachers' efforts to aid those youngsters were frustrated and subverted. Mr. Ford then retired as building principal, and the new principal was asked to confront the problem.

GUIDELINES

1. Principals should establish a collegial relationship with the school's teaching faculty to make the education of their charges as successful as possible.

2. Students should receive rational, insightful and personalized counseling and guidance concerning the courses they may take.
3. The role of ombudsman, if it is to be established, should have clearly defined responsibilities.
4. Teachers, counselors, chairpersons, ombudsman—all staff members—should focus on the needs of each student. Self-fulfillment or advancement develop most easily from a pattern of professional giving.
5. It is the principal's responsibility to be certain that adopted guidelines (1-4) are followed by all staff members.

SITUATION 3

PROBLEM: Initiating a Mandated Program with a Partially Reluctant Staff

SITUATION: Interoffice Memorandum

by
Gene Geisert

TO: Betty Hill, Assistant Superintendent for Instruction
FROM: Mike Keen, Superintendent
SUBJECT: <u>Complaints Concerning Phase-in of Mastery Learning Program</u>

Three different Board members mentioned that they received telephone calls from parents complaining about the proposed phase-in of the Mastery Learning Program we re-

> cently adopted as the result of a Board policy decision to use that process to respond to the differing academic levels and styles of our student population.
>
> The calls appear to have been stimulated by some of our veteran teachers at the high school. Please look into the matter and take appropriate steps to allay their fears and gain their support.

Betty Hill reached for the phone and used the direct line to Herb Starr, the high school principal. Herb, ever on top of things, already knew and had tried to reach her earlier. He agreed to come to her office right after dismissal time.

Betty and Herb carefully reviewed the change strategy that had been developed to insure an effective implementation of the Mastery Learning Program. The program was to be the cornerstone of the district plan to improve student achievement and success. These were critical factors in the attempt to regain community support for budget approvals, badly needed support staff and building rehabilitation.

Betty instinctively knew that the superintendent's job would be very much "on the line" pending an assessment of the Mastery Learning Program's eventual impact on achievement scores. She was supportive of the program, and she certainly wanted to protect Dr. Keen's position in the district. Herb was an advocate of both, too; in addition, he had four years until retirement and wanted to reverse what seemed to him to be a softening in standards at the High School.

During the initial teacher workshops, Betty had observed a clique of veteran teachers who seemed rather hostile toward the consultants; at the time she had considered their remarks as being representative of resentment toward an outsider who had chided them on the comparative lack of learner success in the district. Herb remembered the group and noted that he could list each of their names. He admitted that he hadn't been very concerned about their reactions at those first few sessions; he certainly thought they'd give the program a fair change. Now, however, it was possible that a concerted effort to discredit the program was at the center of those teachers' hostile behavior.

On reflection, Betty also considered that another part of their hidden agenda might be to cause the program to fail and ultimately to embarrass (and thus get rid of) the young superintendent who

FUNCTIONING EFFECTIVELY WITH THE CENTRAL OFFICE

was hired specifically to shake up the district and to reverse the downhill academic trend that appeared to be developing into a pattern.

Herb concurred and reported that the same group had been urging him to "take it easy and enjoy the last few years before retirement." "After all," they'd rejoined, "we built this school's reputation, and we're entitled to some peace and stability; and so are you, Herb!" His appeals to their professionalism and the needs of the students were rejected. "Who's gonna appreciate all that effort?" they retorted.

KEY ISSUES

A. Can a principal persuade recalcitrant veteran teachers about the wisdom of anything new if there is a predisposition toward rejection of anything other than the status quo?

B. What strategies can be employed to initiate promising programs, mandated or otherwise, despite partial or substantive opposition?

C. How can the principal gain the support and assistance of the central office for programs of mutual concern?

ANALYSIS AND ACTION

Betty and Herb agreed on a strategy, and Betty dictated a confidential memo to the superintendent outlining their approach.

CONFIDENTIAL MEMORANDUM

TO: Dr. Michael Keen
FROM: Betty Hill and Herb Starr
SUBJECT: Phase-in of Mastery Learning Program

Herb Starr and I both agree that the most critical technical requirement for installing a district-wide Mastery Learning Program is that every teacher be qualified and committed to this approach, particularly at the high school where the largest pocket of resistance appears to exist.

When such a commitment is lacking, disapproving teachers will tend <u>not</u> to use the new professional practices required for the successful implementation of the adopted concept.

> In our estimation, approximately one-third of our teaching staff at the high school is eagerly awaiting the implementation of the Mastery approach. Another third is believed to have adopted a cautious "wait and see" attitude; the final third (which in our district for various reasons, tends to be veteran teachers) adamantly opposes the move. The overall percentage appears to be much more favorable toward the change at our junior high and elementary schools.
>
> In view of the above, Herb and I suggest that you consider a gradual phase-in of the program, selecting only the most interested and committed teachers for the first stages. The consultants have agreed to concentrate their efforts and provide the Phase I teachers with thorough and intensified training which would enable them to learn, apply and share with others the new learner-centered practices.
>
> These "key" teachers would be most likely to ensure the successful implementation of the program. Once this approach achieves success (i.e., achievement scores significantly improve next year), the second group of teachers could be brought on board. We believe that by the third year it will be very difficult for any teachers to fight the successes we anticipate.
>
> Herb also wants to assure you that some veteran teachers are in the positively disposed group.
>
> While I realize that our recommendation requires a three-year time frame, I believe it represents the best course of action to break down the present negative buildup and still permit us to move forward with a good chance of eliciting widespread faculty support.

The superintendent accepted the two administrators' strategy and rejected negotiation, strong memos, team meetings and various other approaches; he believed that their careful assessment of the situation and suggested course of action had the best chance for success.

In any new program there are unavoidable problems with implementation procedures and unplanned delays that frustrate both teachers and administrators. Each provocation would reawaken criticisms from teachers who still prefer to do things their way.

The administration decided to take the time needed and to encourage the strongest teacher/principal teams at both the high

FUNCTIONING EFFECTIVELY WITH THE CENTRAL OFFICE 31

school and other buildings to begin the new process in ways that would promote success.

GUIDELINES

1. Listen very carefully to all faculty members as they react to changes or new programs. Assess attitudes, but do not spend time on motives; actions or behaviors are what are central to the success of any change.
2. Work closely and candidly with the central office personnel given responsibility for programs, projects and changes.
3. Consider options that will guarantee success. Involve able, motivated staff who are determined to make a project work.
4. Use the variables of time, location, personnel and support from the central office wisely to initiate and sustain new programs.

SITUATION 4

> PROBLEM: Using Professional Consultants
>
> SITUATION: Responding to Direction from the Central Office

by
Richard Sinatra

The superintendent directed the principal of the Springfield Elementary School to redesign the reading program in an effort to raise state basic skills test scores. The school had been focusing on a basal reading series and "ability" reading groups—a traditional approach that had served its pupils well for many years but that no longer obtained the same high scores.

Jim Renzo, the principal, knew that the student body had changed; basic intelligence was lower and interest in academics seemed to have declined. He knew that two professors at a local university had been working on an instrument that determines what occurs during the time span when reading is taught. The next morning Jim called Bob Roberts, one of the researchers, for an appointment. During their meeting that week, Roberts explained that a great deal of time, energy and often heated argument in a school is spent on comparing the merits of one curriculum program against another—even though the rationale and procedures of each approach might be similar. Instead of making program judgments and initiating curriculum changes based on minor distinctions between product format and content, administrators should look at what occurs during the teaching of content. After all, with reading in particular, researchers have provided conflicting data. Some report that it is the *teacher* and not the method that makes the difference (Artley, 1972); or that it is the faculty, *under the leadership of the principal*, systematically using a system in which they have become competent and in which they have confidence, that makes a difference in a school's achievement (Singer, 1977); or that the correct matching of a complementary approach and the student's perceptual strengths produces increased reading achievement (Urbschat, 1977; Carbo, 1980; and Wheeler, 1980); or that students who are taught through their individual learning styles evidence statistically significant increased reading speed and comprehension scores (Pizzo, 1981; Krimsky, 1982).

Roberts went on: "Investigations conducted during the mid-70s, seeking answers to the question of which instructional variables most influenced student achievement, revealed some startling findings that are highly important for principals and curriculum supervisors to consider. First, a positive relationship exists between instructional time allocated to a curriculum area and student achievement (Fisher, et.al., 1976). Teachers control and allocate their own time in the teaching process and direct students in ways which strongly influence and condition the kinds and degrees of their active learning. However, when allocated time was compared against 'engaged' student time (the actual amount of time in which youngsters really concentrate on the task) in reading and mathematics, it was found that many second graders were engaged in reading activities only about fifty percent of the time allocated to reading (Fisher, et.al., 1976), and fifty percent of the time allocated to math (Filby, 1977)."

Moreover, Filby reported that sustained reading time was remarkably low in some classes, with as little as 15 minutes per day actually devoted to reading. In another report by Fisher, et.al. (1978), it was noted that the average engagement rate for second and fifth graders in reading and math was between 70 and 75 percent. However, those authors believed that the higher engagement rate occurred because they did not exclude "transition activities" such as student movement and waiting time from the allocated reading and math time as was done in other studies.

Recently, Stallings (1980) reported, after observing 87 secondary school remedial reading classes, that it is not only a question of how much time is allocated, but also how that time is used. "Interactive verbal activities like reading aloud and class discussion, along with positive, corrective feedback, were highly related to the success of less able students."

"You see, Jim," Roberts continued, "these findings were based on very detailed observations of teachers and students during instruction over a period of time. By synthesizing many of the observational procedures used in several studies, I am now able to provide principals and curriculum supervisors a means of objectively quantifying how teachers and students spend their time during reading instruction."

KEY ISSUES

   A. Should curriculum or program change be attempted by staff and principal without outside assistance?
   B. If outside assistance is sought, how should it be selected?
   C. Who should be involved from *within* the school?
   D. What should the principal do to ensure pilot program success?
   E. Where contradictory research exists, shouldn't the principal seek alternative sources and reports?

ANALYSIS AND SOLUTIONS

Jim liked what Roberts had to say; he was impressed with the way the researcher blended data and the practical aspects of day-today teaching. Roberts outlined an approach for beginning a pilot program to assess what was actually happening when reading was taught in Jim's building. Jim advised that he would form a faculty group to consider the venture and would get back to Roberts in a couple of weeks.

Teachers at each grade level were invited to form a committee to consider the superintendent's directive and Roberts' proposal to implement a pilot program to assess what was actually occurring during the periods allocated to reading. Jay Perrin, a primary teacher, looked puzzled. "I don't see the direct relationship between the need for a redesigned reading program and monitoring how the time is being spent on reading when it is being taught," she posed. "There *is* a relationship between the two," countered Bee Gardiner, "but what is revealed will not necessarily indicate whether we ought to change our reading books and other resources, the amount of time we spend on reading, what we do during that time, and which kids need more or less time on the topic or different materials or methods. This is an unfocused approach; or, rather, it is focused in a direction different from what I would have considered!" The sixth grade teacher continued. "Frankly, I took a course with Roberts while I was getting my master's degree, and although he quotes research, I always kind of felt he was a bit off target. He *sounds* practical, but he's somewhere up in space!"

Jim was taken aback. Had Roberts misdirected his attention? He asked the other members of the group for their opinions.

Jay Perrin suggested that Jim tell Roberts that the committee had decided to investigate other possibilities before making a commitment to the pilot program as described by the researcher. She then added that it might be advantageous for each committee member to assume the responsibility for looking up the studies that Roberts had mentioned, just to get a feeling for the topic. She also remembered a Professor Carbo who had impressed her when she spoke at the National Association for Supervision and Curriculum Development Annual Conference the previous year. Carbo had advocated "matching reading approaches to students' perceptual strengths."

Jim remembered Roberts talking about Carbo's work and thought it *would* be a good idea to pursue that particular line.

A fourth grade teacher had heard about Lynch's study on time of day and volunteered to follow through on that at the local library. Another person said he'd call the major book publishers and share their concerns about the need for a new program, requesting that either copies of new offerings be forwarded to the school for examination and/or that a representative be sent to discuss the matter.

Patty Bren said that she'd contact the International Reading Association president and request guidelines for the adoption of new texts, and at the same time, Helena Hode exploded with, "Maybe we shouldn't consider a *text* or *series* at all! I read an article that described a great New York City school that improved the reading levels of delinquent teenagers by using very high interest materials instead of books! Let me locate that publication, and I'll bring it in! Let's consider *really* good alternatives! Let's do it right if we're putting all this effort into it!"

GUIDELINES

1. Outside assistance is necessary if options are to be available and if newer concepts are to be considered.
2. Professionals within the school must be involved if on-target suggestions are to be incorporated successfully into any emerging program.
3. Involvement of staff often produces "ownership" of an idea or practice. It is wise to bring teachers into the discussion and planning at a beginning stage.
4. Consider many possible sources of information before adopting any new idea, practice, materials and so forth. Most people become involved in their own areas of concentration and often do not keep up with what is happening in other aspects of the field.
5. *Test* any program or materials that you are considering adopting with the actual children for whom they are intended. A pilot program is always a good idea before widespread adoption or purchase.
6. A central approach should be established for each pilot program. Experimental projects should focus on variables that can be monitored and evaluated; e.g., use of interest-based materials, diagnosis and prescription based on learning styles, learning to read through writing.

REFERENCES

A. S. Artley, "The Teacher Variable in the Teaching of Reading," in *The First R: Readings on Teaching Reading*, ed. by C. J. Wallen and S. Sebesta. Chicago, Illinois: Science Research Associates, Inc. (1972).

Marie Antonetti Carbo, "An Analysis of the Relationships Between the Modality Preferences of Kindergartners and Selected Reading Treatments As They Affect the Learning of a Basic Sight-Word Vocabulary," Ed.D. Dissertation, St. John's University (1980).

Nikola N. Filby, et al., *Allocated and Engaged Time in Different Content Areas of Second and Fifth Grade Reading and Mathematics Curriculum* (1977) : 29 (ED 137 315).

Charles W. Fisher, et al., *A Study of Instructional Time in Grade 2 Reading. Technical Report 11-4, BTES (Beginning Teacher Evaluation Study)* (1976) : 201 (ED 145 414).

Charles W. Fisher, et al., *Selected Findings from Phase III BTES. (Beginning Teacher Evaluation Study)* (1978) : 172 (ED 160 639).

Jeffrey Krimsky, "A Comparative Study of the Effects of Matching and Mismatching Fourth Grade Students With Their Learning Style Preference For the Environmental Element of Light and Their Subsequent Reading Speed and Accuracy Scores," Ed.D. Dissertation, St. John's University (1982).

Jeanne Pizzo, "An Investigation of the Relationships Between Selected Acoustic Environments and Sound, an Element of Learning Style, As They Affect Sixth Grade Students' Reading Achievement and Attitudes," Ed.D. Dissertation, St. John's University (1981).

Harry Singer, "Resolving Curricular Conflicts in the 1970's: Modifying the Hypothesis, It's the Teacher Who Makes the Difference in Reading Achivement." *Language Arts* 54 (February 1977) : 158-163.

Jane Stallings, "Allocated Academic Learning Time Revisited, or Beyond Time on Task," *Educational Researcher* 9 (December 1980) : 11-16.

Karen Spangenberg Urbschat, "A Study of Preferred Learning Modes and Their Relationship to the Amount of Recall of CVC Trigrams," Ph.D. Dissertation, Wayne State University (1977).

Roberta Wheeler, "An Alternative to Failure: Teaching Reading According to Students' Perceptual Strengths," *Kappa Delta Pi Record* 17, 2 (December, 1980) : 59-63.

Child Behaviors	Adult Behaviors
1. Students did not ask to use the outdoor facilities.	1. There had been no attempt to train parent volunteers.
2. Children did not use the instructional areas correctly.	2. The teachers did not use parent volunteers at all.
3. Children did not organize their learning materials.	3. The staff did not take advantage of the outdoor facilities.
4. Students did not take care of, share or repair materials.	4. The staff had not unpacked and sorted boxes of materials before school opened.
5. Students did not use the special equipment and supplies.	5. The staff had not organized the materials for learning experiences.
6. Students seemed to rely heavily on reading as the main form of learning or relaxation.	6. The teachers did not train pupils to work with objectives, select from among approved alternatives, follow through on options, assess themselves, etc.
7. Students selected their own curriculum all the time.	7. Carpet squares were not used appropriately, or at all by teachers.
8. Children read silently to themselves; no small group work or tutoring occurred.	8. Teachers did not coordinate student activities.
9. Students worked independently all the time, never with a partner, peers or groups.	9. Teachers did not give students prescriptions of any kind.
10. Students worked according to their own interests without regard to their aptitudes, needs or skills.	10. Open space was not utilized properly by teachers for appropriate instructional areas.
11. Resources were not used much.	11. Learning activities seemed spontaneous but without any direction from teachers.
12. Children did not use media equipment.	12. Teachers used plan books and did not provide individual prescriptions.
13. Children determined their own learning activities and use of resources without direction most of the time.	13. Teachers used instructional time to unpack and examine supplies.

Child Behaviors	Adult Behaviors
14. Self-selection of activities seemed independent and focused primarily on reading or drawing.	14. Student teachers were not participating in instruction during class time.
15. The children's learning activities were not integrated with any topic or field.	15. Aides were doing secretarial chores.
16. Children did not assess their own work.	16. Teachers were not required to correct inappropriate teaching techniques.
17. The pupils did not work in accord with their learning styles.	17. The teachers planned for two and three weeks in advance without diagnosing, evaluating or establishing an appropriate instructional environment.
18. Children did not report to any one concerning work they had completed.	18. Teachers did not describe their program correctly; open education, the British Primary School or the integrated day were not accurate.
	19. The staff did not recognize that some students require a great deal of structure and that most students require some.

B. Major problems and recommendations (approved by staff and parent groups).

Problems	Procedures to Improve the Teaching-Learning Situation
1. Staff misunderstanding of open education, integrated day, etc.	1. In-service workshops and continuing planning with aides, principal and student teachers.
2. Lack of an effective individualized approach.	2. Program to develop diagnoses, prescriptions, organized resources, learning activities, reporting alternatives, evaluation, etc. (entire staff).

FUNCTIONING EFFECTIVELY WITH THE CENTRAL OFFICE

Problems	Procedures to Improve the Teaching-Learning Situation
3. Poor utilization of space, indoors and out.	3. Redesign of instructional areas, correct placement of bookcases and other furniture, establishment of alcoves for small groups; development of appropriate resources at learning stations, interest centers, media corners, etc.
4. Lack of objectives, diagnoses, prescriptions and assessment.	4. Use of consultants and workshops to accomplish the redesign.
5. Non-use of media and resources.	5. Use of aides and secretaries, with librarian and media specialist, to establish media corners, materials at different levels, multisensory resources, etc.
6. Non-use of volunteer parents.	6. Workshops for parents and all other interested community personnel.

GUIDELINES

1. A newly appointed principal should be sensitive to the contributions and methods of previous administrators and their relationships to the Central Office and the community.
2. Defensiveness can usually be overcome by directness, warmth, sincerity, sensitivity and enthusiasm for improving upon existing programs and structures.
3. Involvement of all concerned in open, joint assessment and planning promotes ownership, trust and motivation.
4. Specific assessment of what students do and produce, and what teachers do with and for students provides insights for improvement.

2
Working with Boards of Education

OH, MAN! WHAT'S ON THE AGENDA?! SALARIES? BUDGET CUTS? MY HEAD?

SITUATION 6

PROBLEM: Reaching Goals for Students Through Policy Decisions

SITUATION: Program Value Dispute

by
Barbara Shay

George P. is a data processing teacher and a faculty advisor for the student Vocational Club in the A. Z. Technical High School. Each year, students throughout the state compete with others for recognition of developing skills in their particular trade areas. Leadership and "Best Club" competitions also are sponsored. Winning students continue the competition in a national contest with other state finalists.

The Vocational Club was created originally to provide students with a sense of achievement and pride in their technical areas and to help develop leadership skills through a club organized and conducted according to standard parliamentary procedure. School elections, campaigns and other activities of student government, such as those in academic high schools, also are conducted.

Mr. P. is an enthusiastic advisor and works with students who compete in the data processing area with the intensity of a coach preparing for a national debating contest.

Mr. A., a counselor for the technical school, approached Mr. P. to discuss the activities for the upcoming contest. Mr. A. was concerned that several students had not been attending regular classes for the past few weeks because of their involvement in practice for "Prepared Speech." The students were average to above average, but Mr. A. thought that another two to three weeks of such irregular attendance would affect their learning and perhaps influence their attitudes toward the need for class attendance in the future.

Mr. P. thought Mr. A.'s attitude was "ridiculous" and that practice was necessary to secure First Place. "I want to make sure these kids know their stuff inside out, and this is the way to do it! They'll catch up in their other work. *All* my D.P. (Data Processing) students have been practicing for this contest! So what if they're not all competing? They all have school spirit and are enjoying helping the ones who will compete!"

Mr. A. indicated that clubs are not supposed to take students away from their regular lessons and that some adjustments needed to be made to insure that the students would not fall behind in their class work.

Mr. P. responded that Mr. A. had no school spirit and should see the principal if he had a problem. Immediately thereafter, Mr. A. made an appointment to see Ms. D., the principal. He expressed his concerns regarding the role of extracurricular activities in relation to the students' total school program.

He believed that the club activities were an important addition to the students' program, but that winning contests should not become the main objective of schooling. "If such an attitude became prevalent," he added, "little other learning would take place, and that could adversely affect a student's overall attitudinal development. Academic performance in regular classes should take precedence over competitions."

Ms. D. assured Mr. A. that she would check into the situation, but reminded him that winning a national contest would certainly bring prestigious recognition for the school. "That could help when funds are requested and proposals submitted to the state. These are things that must be considered as well."

KEY ISSUES

A. How carefully has the Board of Educaton developed policies that reflect its collective decisions regarding instructional goals?
B. In this situation, have the values of cocurricular and extracurricular experiences been defined carefully and relationships to the regular program established?

C. Whether policies deal with areas in dispute or not, how well has the school faculty analyzed and developed school rules and procedures dealing with important instructional considerations?

ANALYSIS

Decisions on broad instructional issues are properly the province of the Board of Education. For example, general statements about instructional goals, the value of cocurricular and extracurricular activities, and their relative relationship to the overall program should be developed with assistance from the superintendent's office, the principals and designated teachers.

In this situation, the principal should develop her school's position on this issue and follow with cooperatively written procedures concerning released time from classes, make-up sessions and all procedures dealing with cocurricular activities.

Should students be excused from their regular class schedule to participate in all club activities, rehearsals or parties? It would seem that this would be violating the students' rights to an education. Specific, occasional interruptions can be justified, but to have students miss numerous classes to participate in those activities, without regard to what is being missed in class, cannot.

School spirit and winning are certainly positive goals for students. Football teams and debate teams, for example, are hailed for placing first. Team members in those activities do not miss academic classes to practice. Winning contests and school prestige or recognition should not be overriding priority goals in an educational system. Education is for all students, and their individual goals should be of primary importance.

Nevertheless, contests, competitions and/or experiences in other locations with student counterparts and state or national judges can become an important adjunct, if not the central focus of the curriculum. Involving most, if not all, students in those activities—with appropriate scheduling—could be of major benefit to the school's educational goals.

GUIDELINES

1. Schools should request Boards of Education to establish broad policies dealing with educational goals.

2. Principals should work with the faculty in developing procedures and rules for the day-to-day implementation of Board policy.
3. All programs should begin with specific objectives and outcomes against which to measure student progress; evaluation should be an ongoing process.
4. Qualitative and quantitative differences should be detailed for various types of co-curricular and extracurricular programs. For example, data processing clubs that provide enrichment experiences for gifted students would receive a higher priority than a club planning a social event; a technological "fair" for all students would be more important than an activity involving five students.

SITUATION 7

PROBLEM: Coping with Board Members Who Try to Administer a Principal's Building

SITUATION: Visits and Confrontations

by
John Spiridakis

Two newly elected members of a nine-member urban school Board have been pressing in subtle (and sometimes not so subtle) ways for principals of schools that they serve as liaison members to adopt some of their approaches to education.

One of the Board members, Dr. Dubious, a chiropractor, is a strong advocate of the back-to-basics program in education, and at various meetings with Mr. Mildew, principal of P.S. 500, has indicated his displeasure at the principal's failure to adopt a strict phonics approach to the teaching of reading. He points out to the principal that P.S. 600, which does utilize a phonics approach, has much higher reading scores than P.S. 500. Dr. Dubious visits the building at least once a week and calls the principal, the superintendent and other Board members regularly about this "terrible gap in the spine of our reading program. It's something we must straighten out," he repeats. He uses any test data that has been published to support his view—whether relevant or not.

A second Board member, Mrs. Letitia Fair, a graduate of prestigious Grinn More College, is a proponent of the open classroom, and on her tour of P.S. 700, comments in no uncertain terms to its principal, Mrs. Strick (who is newly appointed and on probation) that the silent halls and quiet classrooms connote a sterile educational program lacking in the vitality that growing younsters exude. She reinforces this conviction at subsequent meetings with the principal and also with the Executive Board of the school's Parent/Teachers Association. Mrs. Fair bombards Board members, the principal and the PTA with articles that easily could be interpreted as being supportive of open approaches—whether applicable to P.S. 700 or not.

KEY ISSUES

A. How does Mr. Mildew, principal of P.S. 500, justify his reading program while avoiding invidious comparisons with his colleague at P.S. 600 or elsewhere?

B. How does Mrs. Strick defend her traditional school to so ardent an advocate of the open classroom as Mrs. Fair?

C. How do principals who disagree with the opinions of individual Board members communicate those differences without causing offense and without indicating their continuing awareness that their superintendent must submit his ratings and recommendations for continued employment to those same people?

D. In the long range, how does a building principal work with the superintendent and the Board in aiding individual Board members to understand and observe their roles as those who deal wisely with broad policy issues as a unit and not as individuals?

ANALYSIS

Initial discussion must be held between each principal and Board of Education members assigned as liaison by the Board. An objective and professional rationale should be offered for a particular program or approach. Performance results and research data should be provided to buttress professional decisions.

The superintendent should be contacted at the first sign of either intervention or disagreement. A Board member's attempted involvement in administrative decisions is inappropriate, but decorum and professionalism are always advisable regardless of the impropriety of the Board members' intrusion.

It is hoped that the superintendent will have the personal strength and resolution to deal with this type of problem directly with the Board—but usually through its president. Board members who work together usually resolve such problems far more effectively than superintendents who may have to confront Board members' inappropriate behaviors directly.

Education of new Board members through state or national organization workshops is an effective way to focus attitudes on broad policy issues instead of on selected building programs. On the positive side, issues raised by individual Board members can be used to develop forums in which principals can lead discussions and staff presentations to support current programs, request assistance, urge new budget priorities and so on.

GUIDELINES

1. Always react to Board members with politeness and professionalism.
2. Work closely with the superintendent as soon as inappropriate interference or pressure becomes apparent.
3. Prepare in-depth supporting evidence for any program that is challenged or potentially subject to future assessment by the superintendent or Board.
4. Work for opportunities to join the superintendent and Board at meetings at which programs of direct concern are to be weighed and decisions made.
5. Recommend workshops, if they don't already exist, for new Board members and principals, too, if coping skills should be sharpened.

SITUATION 8

> **PROBLEM:** Dealing with Divided or Misguided Board Members
>
> **SITUATION:** Negotiations Sabotage: A Timely Phone Call

by
Gene Geisert

Negotiations centering around a salary increase for the second year of a two-year contract began in earnest in mid-August. The Board's stated position to the superintendent, which was announced publicly, was that no salary increases were to be offered. The Teachers' Union was adament that until a reasonable money offer was made, it would not return to the bargaining table. To emphasize that position, a strike vote was taken and approved by an overwhelming majority of the membership.

After 10 days of holding to their "no increase" position, the Board decided to use "budgeted surplus" funds for the salary increases and authorized the superintendent and the negotiating team to make an opening offer of $800,000 to the teachers. The Union rejected the offer as being too low, and negotiations broke off again with the Board accusing the Union of moving too slowly, and the Union accusing the Board of insulting them with "nickel-and-dime offers."

It was at this point, two days before the opening of school, that the superintendent, Jim Smith, received a confidential phone call from his high school principal, Ed Jones, a member of the Board's negotiating team. The conversation transpired as follows:

"Hello, Jim Smith speaking."

WORKING WITH BOARDS OF EDUCATION

"Hi, Jim. This is Ed. Are you free to talk?"

"Yes. What's up?"

"What I'm about to tell you is in strictest confidence. I'm sharing this information with you only because I believe we're headed for a strike that will hurt students and tear the community apart. The only reason I found out is that one of my best teachers, a member of the Union team, doesn't want a strike either, and what he observed so disgusted him that he called me. Jim, the reason for our inability to gain any movement toward a settlement is that one of our own Board members met secretly with the president of the Union and agreed to give the teachers whatever they want. Every step of your negotiations is known by the Union in advance. This rear guard action is so serious that unless something is done immediately, our team will lose all credibility at the bargaining table, and we'll be unable to reach any settlement prior to the scheduled opening of school."

"Ed, thank you for taking me into your confidence. I'll keep you out of this, but, obviously, I've got to do something quickly. Thank you for your call."

"Good luck, Jim!"

KEY ISSUES

A. How does a principal deal with confidential and potentially dangerous information?

B. What level of trust and understanding must exist between a principal and the superintendent to deal with difficult situations in complete candor?

C. How does a superintendent deal with a Board and staff in matters of inappropriate action and simultaneously maintain harmony and credibility with all concerned?

D. How should unethical behavior be dealt with when confidentiality must be maintained?

ANALYSIS

Jim hung up the phone and pondered his options. How do you deal with a Board member who is personally undercutting management and the other Board members regardless of the motives?

Jim asked for a special executive session of the Board to assert publicly that *only* the chief negotiator, the superintendent in this case, had the authority to make offers that were binding, and reaffirmed the role of the negotiating team as the *sole* representative body when bargaining for the Board.

The Board president was asked to read the adopted resolution before a press conference, and Jim conveyed the substance of the Board's action personally to the Union president. With clear lines of communication reestablished between management's negotiation team and the Union, the State Mediator was able to resolve the dispute before the scheduled strike deadline.

Ed, the high school principal, and a member of the district's negotiating team, had acted responsibly in informing the superintendent of the inappropriate action of the Board member. Jim, the superintendent, had reasoned correctly that a direct confrontation with an individual Board member would only serve to further divide management in the face of a united Union. Instead, he forced the Board to overrule one of its own members without identifying the guilty party, thereby preserving a unified front and gaining the vote of confidence he needed to resolve the dispute.

GUIDELINES

1. A principal has two basic sets of allegiance: (a) to the students, his staff and the school system; and (b) to the superintendent and the Board of Education.
2. His or her course of action should be predicated on mutual respect, trust and agreement on procedures that are ethical and in the best interests of students and the school system.
3. Sensitive areas, wherein people in authority do not understand or abuse their position, attempt to influence decisions for personal reasons, or divide a group after agreeing to a specific position, must be dealt with immediately but with astute professionalism and awareness of the potential consequences of either no action or precipitous, nonproductive confrontation.

SITUATION 9

> PROBLEM: Planning for Board of Education Visits to Your Building
>
> SITUATION: Take Them Where the Action Is

by
Rita Dunn and Kenneth Dunn

The entrance hall of the Community School Building in Whitmore, New York, was empty and dark when Meredith Kane entered at 9:30 Monday morning. "No one's here again," she mused. "I must be dumb to believe that the kids will be here and anxious to learn on Monday morning!" She stepped inside, turned on the lights to the inner lounge area and stepped into the office with the day's mail in her hands.

She heard steps just outside the door, and Meredith's heart jumped! "It's happened at last," she thought. "Some kid cared enough to drag himself out of bed before noon!" She turned quickly toward the door in anticipation, only to find Will Brewster, the school's principal.

"Don't look so disappointed," Will laughed. "Were you expecting students?" Meredith nodded. "What went wrong with this program, Will? We planned it so well! Administrative support! Community support! Direct student and teacher involvement! How could any venture so lovingly designed fall apart so quickly and thoroughly?"

"Have you read the 'Village School' story?" Brewster asked. "It takes time ... "

"Time for what?"

"Time for kids to realize they want to learn. Starting a community school is only exciting at the beginning. It takes a lot of work to get over the dull, difficult, uninteresting moments as well as the apathy and minor problems."

"Like getting out of bed before noon so that classes might begin on time occasionally?" Meredith asked. "Or remaining through one whole course?" She sighed in exasperation. "I think we've made a dreadful mistake," she said. "These students weren't ready for the kind of freedom we gave them!"

"Maybe not," Will replied. "But maybe we weren't ready for their use of freedom in a way with which we didn't agree!"

"We spent two years listening to their gripes about the irrelevant curriculum, the mandatory classes, the meaningless assignments, the dull teachers and the restrictive regulations at the high school 'prison'," she retorted. "Throughout that entire period I had the distinct impression that if they could study what they themselves chose, attend classes at times that they determined, demonstrate their knowledge in ways other than tests or assignments, and select their own teachers, they'd become model students. Well, they were given all of that! Now where are they? They rarely arrive before noon, are too lazy to attend the very classes they designed, and are too unmotivated to stay with the teachers *they* selected for more than four or five sessions! I predict that the Board and the community will react against this lack of self-discipline and abort the entire experiment. And frankly, I don't feel it's worth continuing."

Brewster considered her "speech" soberly. "I understand your reactions. Perhaps we should have prepared the students to design and select courses more carefully than they did, and helped them to see their choices through."

"On the other hand, wouldn't that have detracted from our efforts to aid young people to mature by giving them decision-making power as they see the need?" she asked.

"Mature young people also most assume the responsibility for carrying through on decisions they make," Will replied. "Maybe it's not too late for this group. Could we build some of these elements into our structure now? Would the students buy it?"

"Buy what?" asked a young, vivacious girl in blue jeans and a white knit body suit who had just entered the lounge. "What are you and Meredith so upset about?"

"Yes, why are people upset?" asked John Nelson and Jill Dawson, two Board members who had been invited to visit the Community School by the superintendent and the principal. They had walked in with the student.

Meredith and Will turned to greet Janey, a junior in the high school who had just entered the Community School this past term, and the two Board members.

John Nelson, the Board member, spoke earnestly as he shook their hands. "We came to understand and to help if we could."

"Yes," added Jill Dawson. "We believe in the concept of the Community School, but if some structure and self-control aren't exhibited soon, we will have to discontinue it."

KEY ISSUES

A. How does a principal gain support for a new program from Board members?

B. How does a principal involve students in decisions affecting their program of learning?

C. How can a principal provide structure, eliminate apathy and build motivation?

ANALYSIS

"We've been talking about some of the problems of the school as we see them," Will answered, "and were wondering whether we could gain student support for some reforms."

"Like what?" Janey asked.

"Like permitting free selection of courses, but then, after the selection, have mandatory attendance for the length of the course—or at least until a certain point."

Janey's face brightened. "That would be good," she said. "Then courses wouldn't break up because some kids got tired of the subject before the rest of us had a chance to really get into it! What else?"

"We don't know what else," said Will. "Any suggestions?"

Janey thought. "Some of the kids are doing great work out of classes," she answered. "They shouldn't have to attend meetings if they can show they know what the rest of the kids are studying. They could take a test or give a report." Her eyes lit up as she warmed to the idea. "Maybe they could *teach* the part they know. After all, we all like to learn or show what we know in different ways."

"That's a neat idea," said Meredith. "We could ask—require—that each student file a list of learning objectives to be completed and the way in which the knowledge or skills acquired could be demonstrated. Students also could submit a list of resources that they used in learning. In that way we'd know their sources of information and could suggest others if theirs seem biased or inadequate."

Will was getting caught up in the enthusiasm. "How will we evaluate their learning if they use resources that we haven't seen ourselves?" he questioned.

"We can evaluate their learning on the basis of completed activities they ought to design by themselves. They could actually use the information they've learned in a creative way and then, perhaps, share it with some of the other students and us. They could evaluate their own progress, and the products of their classmates, and we could do both too. You know," Meredith added, "we're really describing contracts—contracts to complete a learning task! Maybe that's what we should have used to begin with—contracts for work-study experiences, for community contribution, for independent study and for the completion of self-selected courses! Why didn't we think of it before? That's what we need for commitment by all concerned."

Will leaned back in his chair and smiled. "If we'd been able to think of everything, there'd be no problems to solve and no need for a principal."

The following week, the students and staff met to list the strengths and weaknesses of the school. They then outlined some ways to achieve improvements.

Strengths	Weaknesses
1. Administrative support	1. Lack of sustained motivation on the part of students
2. Community support	2. Lack of strong expectations by the faculty
3. Student involvement	3. Acceptance of apathy
4. Teacher involvement	4. Lack of reality orientation for all concerned

WORKING WITH BOARDS OF EDUCATION

Strengths	Weaknesses
5. Concerned teachers and director	5. Inappropriate freedom for some
6. Student-selection of curriculum	6. Lack of agreement on types of freedom
7. Alternative means of students demonstrating their knowledge	7. Lack of commitment on the part of students for their own schedules and selections of classes
8. Student-selection of teachers	8. Lack of self-discipline
9. Student-selection of schedule	9. Lack of structure and continuity
10. Student decision-making opportunities	10. Lack of training and readiness for the new approach (both teachers and students)
11. Independent study used	11. Lack of follow-through on decisions
12. Out-of-school studies used	12. Lack of guidelines
13. Bright and creative student participation	13. Lack of assessment
14. Willingness of staff to listen, explore, improve	14. Lack of teaching or reporting interaction among students
	15. Lack of specific objectives and planning of learning.

Major Problems	Recommendations
1. Lack of structure	1. Faculty-student senate to write guidelines with power to adopt and enforce after input from all members of the school
2. Lack of planning, commitment, involvement with others	2. One to two week planning periods to list alternative contracts with specific objectives, alternative learning activities, reporting and teaching alternatives, self- and peer-faculty assessment

Major Problems	Recommendations
3. Inappropriate use of time, lack of motivation, apathy	3. Total school involvement in establishing schedules, courses, options, and out-of-school activities with commitment sought from all through acceptance of self-selected options

Will, Meredith and Janey met with the two Board members after the last Community School planning session.

John Nelson smiled. "I'm really impressed with the students' grasp of the situation. I'm sure Jill and I will have a favorable report on what's happened here this week. Your plans should improve and maintain the community school."

"Yes," Jill Dawson confirmed, "and we would like Janey and some of the other students to join us at a spring Board meeting to describe the school and how students are directly involved in setting goals and evaluating progress."

GUIDELINES

1. Invite Board members to see new programs in action. Have them speak to teachers, administrators and students. Be prepared to describe strengths, weaknesses and plans for improvement.
2. Students at the secondary level should be given choices and options from among approved alternatives. They should have a voice in setting rules, procedures, standards and evaulation.
3. Structure, goals and rules aid in building expectations and improving motivation. Apathy disappears as success increases in the completion of individual and group objectives.

SITUATION 10

> **PROBLEM:** Bridging Relationships Between Schools and Other Educational Units
>
> **SITUATION:** Attendance and Its Relationship to Grades

by
Barbara Shay

Ms. Mary Anderson, Director of the County Intermediate Unit Occupational Center, received a call from the principal of South High School concerning a student's grade. Mr. Jones was irate that Dan Smith, a carpentry student in the occupational center for half of his school day, received an 85% average in the course after being absent for 49 days. The absences were for various reasons including, but not limited to, illness.

Mr. Jones had indicated to all intermediate unit students at the beginning of the school year that attendance was an important factor in achieving good grades in the occupational program. The stressing of good attendance was a result of the pressure he had received from the Board of Education, through the superintendent, who questioned why the district was paying tuition to the intermediate unit for students who were not attending regularly.

Ms. Anderson assured Mr. Jones that the instructor would be contacted and the grade adjusted to reflect attendance; that was a segment of the occupational program's grading policy.

Mr. Brown, the carpentry instructor, indicated to Ms. Anderson when they met that Dan was a very talented student, and added that he had been able to "more than maintain class standards" when he was present, in spite of the absences. He said that Dan had earned the grade even though points had already been deducted for lack of attendance.

The director stated that the grade did not reflect, and was inconsistent with, occupational program policy that stressed employability skills—which included attendance. In fact, good attendance was one of the most important criteria to prospective employers. The grade then was changed to 65%.

Mr. Brown met with the director following distribution of report cards. He still was upset over the grade change. He agreed that attendance is of major importance in the occupational training of students and should be addressed and emphasized as a requisite to continued employment after graduation. However, he also stated that he could not justify the fact that the student's actual performances or skills were being judged partially on the basis of attendance.

Ms. Anderson agreed that it was a sensitive situation but told him that sending districts were concerned with the economics as well as the appropriateness of rewarding poor attendance with good grades, especially in a program stressing employability skills and attitudes. She added that district representatives had expected Dan to receive a failing grade instead of the 65% recorded. Ms. Anderson agreed to arrange for a meeting with district representatives and intermediate unit staff to discuss the issue for recommendation to both Boards of Education.

KEY ISSUES

A. What is the philosophy of grading in the sending district and the intermediate unit?
B. How is this philosophy reflected in each district's Board policy, regulations and school building rules?
C. How are these rules transmitted to principals, supervisors and students?
D. What are the elements of a good grading philosophy?

ANALYSIS

Grades should reflect achievement based on the specific objectives of a given course and should not be modified by criteria dealing with attitudes, behavior, attendance, conformity or other matters not directly related to the performance of the student and the expectations of the teacher.

Obviously, some students can accomplish more in a given time frame than others. However, school districts and individual schools and teachers still tend to use grades as a lever to reward, punish, control and manipulate students along authority-charted paths.

Ideally, schools should establish appropriate objectives through individualized programs based on each student's learning styles, interests, knowledge and skills. Given the current state of the educational establishment, principals should discuss grading philosophy with the staff and prepare position papers for superintendents to recommend to Boards of Education. In cases where more than one Board is involved, meetings to resolve differences should be arranged through their central offices.

GUIDELINES

1. Grades should reflect student performance on clearly stated objectives.
2. Behavioral aspects such as attendance, behavior or attitudes should be reported separately. Criteria for course completion, make-up work or attitude modification should be established apart from student performance on course objectives.
3. Employability profiles can be designed to reflect all aspects of students' potential including their strengths and deficits.
4. Boards should decide on evaluation policies and be informed of district and interdistrict regulations concerning those broad guidelines for action.

3
Enlisting Community Cooperation

SITUATION 11

PROBLEM: Responding to Parental Pressure

SITUATION: Hasty Decision

by
Donal F. Buckley

John Foglia is head track and field coach at Knoxville South High School. During the month of May there were many occasions when he requested that certain members of his team be excused from classes early so that they might attend competitions held a distance from the school. Those competitions usually began in the middle of the school day. In thirteen years of coaching, Mr. Foglia's teams had never been refused permission to leave—until this year of the Southern States Championships.

Exactly two minutes before their scheduled departure, Mr. Foglia called the attendance office to notify the personnel there that he and his team would be leaving; such notification was required by school policy. The secretary stated that the group could not leave because permission had been denied to his previously submitted, written request. The principal was not on the premises; he was attending a National Honor Society Induction ceremony with all the students, their parents and 80 members of the school's band—which had been excused from classes to perform at the ceremony. Mr. Foglia then contacted the assistant principal, but he refused to countermand his superior's decision.

The Southern States Championships annually draws the top track and field athletes from the south; being accepted for this competition is a great honor. When the athletes were told of the principal's decision, they asked if they would be allowed to drive to the competition by themselves. In front of the Director of Athletics, Mr. Foglia told the boys that if they did, they could face grave repercussions. Although warned, the boys held a meeting and decided to leave school and attend the competition anyway. The five boys involved were members of the National Honor Society and had been accepted to the colleges of their choice.

One hour after the boys left, the principal returned to the school. He was told by the assistant principal of the situation, and he rushed to see Mr. Foglia. He demanded to be told the names of the individuals involved and proceeded to call their parents to tell them that their sons would be barred from attending graduation ceremonies. The parents were extremely upset at the principal's decision, and several of them immediately drove to his office.

When the parents began arriving at school, a few stopped to talk with students and were told the details of the situation. Within minutes, that information became known to the entire student body and faculty.

After meeting with the parents, the principal bowed to the pressure and rescinded his order. That change in his original decision also became common knowledge throughout the school.

KEY ISSUES

A. General procedures in place for some time were negated by the principal.
B. There was no communication with those involved.
C. A hasty decision was made to punish students; then the decision was rescinded just as quickly under pressure from the parents concerned.

ANALYSIS

The students involved felt that the principal's decision was unjust. They were all seniors and had been excused from classes many times in the past. Several of them felt that this competition could lead to possible scholarships. They sincerely thought that any disciplinary action taken against them could not be worse than failing to compete in that prestigious meet.

The coach agreed with the students but did not indicate his position to them and, in fact, refused to grant approval. Fearful of possible repercussions against him, he deliberately had the Director of Athletics present when he warned his athletes that they could get into trouble if they went on their own.

The principal's overreaction was unusual, because he was perceived as a laissez-faire administrator. He rarely was seen outside his office, and during times of difficulty he generally looked the other way. He usually allowed the faculty to do whatever they felt was right and rarely made major decisions.

When he returned to the school in this situation, he stepped out of his customary administrative style and tried to take control of the situation. As a result of operating hastily (and unwisely) in a style that was not comfortable for him, he created a situation that was both chaotic and embarrassing. Ironically, this problem would never have occurred if the principal had responded earlier to Mr. Foglia's written request.

In the eyes of the student body and the faculty, the principal further lessened his credibility by reversing his original disciplinary actions in response to parental pressure.

GUIDELINES

1. Answer all requests within an acceptable time frame.
2. Delegate authority and responsibility to assistants in your absence.
3. Provide guidelines and crisis management training for assistants.
4. Reflective consideration and analytic discussion should be planned before important decisions (such as the punitive action in this situation) are made.
5. Consider and weigh extenuating circumstances, specific conditions, traditional practice, timing, consequences and all factors involved before making final decisions—or revising them.

SITUATION 12

> PROBLEM: Establishing Curriculum Advisory Groups
>
> SITUATION: Observing, Meeting, and Deciding—"Flashback"

by
Richard Sinatra

As you escort the officers of the Parent/Teacher Association into the school corridor, you call back to your secretary, "Mrs. Yates, I'm taking the group to observe the kindergarten reading program." Smiling with anticipation, you lead the five-member group down the hall and reminisce about how you were able to achieve program change with veteran teachers while extending the concept of meeting the needs of all children through individualization into the kindergarten curriculum. In this instance you feel that, as principal, you have exercised instructional leadership.

Actually, it all started with a parent request. Some months back you were confronted by an earnest, inquiring parent, Mrs. Baily, who stated that her daughter had been reading before she came to school and that the youngster came home each day reporting that they "just played" in kindergarten. Mrs. Baily also named other parents who felt that the kindergarten experience wasn't satisfying their children's intellectual curiosity. They believed that the school should capitalize on early reading skills before their children became turned off to academic learning.

Assuring the parent that you'd look into the situation, you initially contemplated the dilemma then facing you. You instinctively felt that Mrs. Baily and the others were right in their appraisal of the kindergarten situation, but you also knew that those teachers were a resistant, conservative group who managed the split-session kindergarten classes with efficiency and skill. In the years you had served as principal, no one had introduced a program change or curriculum approach in either your kindergarten or in any of the district's kindergarten classes. A problem had arisen because the kindergarten teachers were mainly concerned with the social and emotional well-being of the youngsters, while the Board, the community and the superintendent embraced the concept of individualization and the provision of alternative programs to respond to the different learning needs of children. Special concern was directed toward classroom situations where children learned and interacted with others. Therefore, multi-aged classes had been formed in the elementary schools throughout the district, beginning with a grade one-two unit in your school. Kindergarten remained the one "untouchable" area. You were torn between action that would destroy the positive school climate it had taken you some years to achieve, and the real concern of providing for all the children's optimal growth.

KEY ISSUES

A. How does a principal promote needed change among a veteran and able group of teachers who are resistant to any variation in their approach to program or instruction?
B. Which staff members and specialists should be involved in the change process?
C. Which strategy approaches are best for involving those directly concerned?

ANALYSIS AND SOLUTIONS

You decided to begin with a low-key plan. You would enlist the advice and support of the school reading specialist who had already earned the respect of the kindergarten teachers by assisting them with readiness materials and techniques for class and parent use. Also, you needed to involve the district's elementary curriculum coordinator in the early stages for program and curriculum input and for articulation among the other schools. At the first meeting, the reading specialist noted that early readers could be easily identified and that assessment was the initial key to finding the number of children who would be involved. After all, if only one or two children were to be involved, major changes in programming would not be necessary. Rather than use a formal testing procedure involving all the kindergartners, the better way to check for early reading proficiency was to listen to a child read orally from a series of graded paragraphs (as in the Informal Reading Inventory procedure) and to check for comprehension of content. In that way, the child's understanding and fluency levels could be obtained. The curriculum coordinator noted that the district had a policy whereby specialists could be released from regular assignments to engage in special task-oriented missions.

The plan adopted was presented as an information-gathering process. The kindergarten teachers were asked to list all the children in their morning and afternoon sessions who showed evidence of positive early reading behaviors. The memo further stated that once all the lists were submitted, the school reading specialist would see each child individually and report her findings to the principal and kindergarten teachers.

Some days later, the reading specialist presented the results to you. The twenty-four children who had been referred to her were classified thus: six children were identified as early readers since they could read paragraphs fluently on as low as the Primer level, and could talk about what they had read. Eleven children had some sight vocabulary but not enough words to read with accuracy at any level. The seven remaining youngsters had a sight vocabulary of one or two words but apparently had good visual discrimination abilities.

In a second conference with the district curriculum coordinator and the reading specialist, you discussed options for presenting the information to the kindergarten teachers and possible strategies for implementing a reading program. It was agreed, however, that if any curriculum changes were to be instituted in kindergarten, the teachers would have to be involved in the decision-making and planning at the outset. Second, while the major focus was directed at the fluent readers and the children with some sight vocabulary, your overall concern was for staff development and attitudinal changes of veteran teachers.

The meetings began with the kindergarten teachers. At first there was great reluctance, even hostility, to implement a formal reading program for children who weren't "socially ready." The teachers thought that there was not enough time in the two and one-half hour session to spend either with individuals or with small groups in a structured manner. However, with continued discussion, especially with input from the reading specialist who showed that a good number of the children were ready for a more challenging academic experience, the overall resistance began to dissipate. The kindergarten teachers agreed that "something had to be done" for most of the identified children, but felt that they didn't have the time, conditions or materials to implement a beginning reading program.

Options and strategies then were considered, such as grouping within the individual rooms; shared grouping led by one kindergarten teacher; the use of parent volunteers, the reading specialist or her assistants to manage groups; the retraining of a paraprofessional who had been assigned another role; employment of a part-time person; and/or allowing the fluent readers to attend reading groups at higher grade levels. Each option had its advantages and disadvantages. Although *you* could have made a clear-cut decision, you were convinced of the merits of continued teacher interaction in curriculum matters and certainly in the reshaping of the kindergarten program.

The final decision reflected a spirit of compromise and willingness to share responsibility in providing for individualized growth. The six fluent readers were to take part in a "Reading-for-Pleasure" program. Since they had already solved some of the mechanical problems associated with decoding, they could continue to read for enjoyment and to gain information. That was arranged for by taking a weekly trip to the library and by spending several periods a week with one of the kindergarten teachers who led oral reading and story-sharing activities. While one teacher was managing the reading groups, the three other kindergarten teachers absorbed her youngsters in other activities. Thus, once a month, each kindergarten teacher had the opportunity to be involved in and to learn the joy of directing the activities of these early readers. Furthermore, those children were encouraged to read aloud to the rest of their classes, acting as peer models for the others to emulate.

The second and larger group of eleven was divided into four rather stable subgroups. A paraprofessional who worked in the elementary reading lab under the direction of the reading specialist was assigned to the kindergarten wing for two twenty-minute periods each morning and afternoon. Since those children had a rather good sight vocabulary, they could begin with the first and second preprimers of the district's basal reading series. The paraprofessional was familiar with the approach of the reading series and rotated her groups weekly into a section of one of the kindergarten rooms, thus receiving input and some direction from each of the kindergarten teachers.

Although the seven remaining children were not placed in a special program, they were identified for the kindergarten teachers as being "most ready" for the reading experience. The teachers decided to use the readiness materials provided for the district's basal reading program for all kindergarten children who were not receiving special assistance. Thus, rather than initiate the formal readiness program in the first few months of first grade, the kindergarten teachers would begin that aspect of the overall reading program and forward the children's unfinished readiness books to their first grade teachers.

As you showed your Parent/Teacher Association officers the different groupings and activities arranged for the kindergarten readers, you felt accomplishment and pride in the way you had helped veteran teachers change their attitudes—particularly since those changes were consistent with a district philosophy of learning in which you strongly believed.

GUIDELINES

1. Involve teachers in a change that affects them directly.
2. Assign specialists who have ability and the respect of those concerned.
3. Demonstrate the needs of individual students (or groups) clearly to professional staff members.
4. Design programs or procedures that are practical, promising and acceptable to the participants.
5. Maintain a communication and evaluation procedure through observation and feedback with those involved.

SITUATION 13

PROBLEM: Dealing with Written Complaints

SITUATION: Letters from Parents

by
Zarif Bacilious

> 18 Hedgewood Lane
> Old Chappan, New York
> 11506
> June 12, 1982
>
> Mr. William Listwell, Principal
> Ring Middle School
> Old Chappan, New York 11506
>
> Dear Dr. Listwell:
>
> I don't want you to intercede in this matter in any way; I merely want you to be aware of what appears to be a consistently insensitive attitude toward youngsters on the part of Miss Strait, the 8th grade science teacher.
> Miss Strait called me this morning and told me that she had asked some of the students to submit a science notebook covering their term's work. She said that Richard's notebook, consisting of some thirty assignments, included two that were taken from another student's book, for the name had been erased and Richard's name superimposed. Perhaps I shouldn't have written "taken," for according to Miss Strait, the other students had "contributed" their papers.

She told me that she had given Richard an F on his entire book as a grade for the term because:
  "...there's a growing immorality around here...,"
  "...the kids here think they can get away with this kind of thing.."
  "...the other teachers see it and don't care.."
  "...I'm concerned about the lack of morals of these kids...and I'm not going to let them get away with this kind of thing..."

I agreed with her that Ricky was completely wrong. I requested, however, that she consider that: (a) she HAD noticed an increasingly improving attitude on Ricky's part; and (b) if two of thirty assignments had been improperly submitted, that she lower his grade proportionately (one level), require that he do the two assignments, speak with him concerning the impropriety of the act, and perhaps require additional work. I suggested than an F for a 1/15th error is excessive and that the punishment far outweighs the crime.

Her grade had already been given and the work returned to Richard. She wouldn't consider the fact that the extreme punishment might not at all achieve the "morality" she wanted; she viewed, instead, that this "...would teach Richard a lesson. He cannot get away with this!"

I don't want you to intercede because I understand what she is trying to do. I want you to be aware because, although a moralist would support her stand, I rather suspect that a humanistic approach to the situation, rather than her penalistic measures, would reap the outcomes she desires.

I suppose it all boils down to a difference in philosophy and approach, but I don't believe that in today's world she is sufficiently sensitive to teenagers and their reactions. Her attitude is authoritarian— "the world is corrupt, and since other teachers are not willing to change it," she will be the super self-righteous savior. It's no wonder that so many of the youngsters feel alienated from her!

Ricky was wrong and should be made to recognize his error, but when the punishment exceeds the crime, it is possible that kids will react negatively, rather than positively. Her entire attitude is so authoritarian and inhumane that I wonder whether she can at all "reach" the kids of today.

At any rate, please keep this letter on file. I think it is necessary to weigh the results of a teacher's attitude and actions on a continuum. I suspect she's outdated for the modus operandi under which youngsters live today. I know that it is

> not easy to change people, but you have been successful with others. Perhaps you can help Miss Strait, and thus her students, at appropriate times in the future.
>
> Sincerely,
>
> Mrs. R. Lange

KEY ISSUES

A. Is Miss Strait's response likely to deter students from cheating as Richard did? Will Richard's behavior change?

B. Did the teacher overreact? Did the punishment fit the crime?

C. Did the teacher consider alternative approaches to the problem? What are some other solutions?

D. Should the principal intercede? Should the teacher be told about the letter? Should the letter go into the teacher's file?

E. Can the principal improve negative or rigid behavior on the part of the staff?

ANALYSIS

A principal should aid teachers in effecting appropriate changes in student behavior. In this case, Richard should learn to resist shortcuts in the completion of an assignment. The "F" would seem to be severe punishment for this infraction. Further, no positive alternatives were considered—simply a failing grade. Additional work, a new chapter in the notebook, helping other students after school, a reduced grade, or any combination of these would probably have produced better results with this student. Motivation and love of learning are not served by excessive punishment; appropriate responses involving the student in make-up work and values discussions are more positive and potentially rewarding approaches.

With respect to the teacher, her emotional, almost puritanical reaction to cheating may be a reflection of hostility based on her own personal problems. This type of assessment must be made with caution, however. Administrators are not psychiatrists.

Nevertheless, principals must develop insights and sensitivity to patterns of teacher behavior that are detrimental to student self-image. Too often, teachers who behave negatively view criticism as a personal attack on their professionalism and demand the principal's loyalty and support even when they have made errors in judgment or have overreacted.

If Miss Strait has a history of repeated responses that coincide with the description in the letter, then counseling and supervision by the principal is in order. If the teacher's reaction reflects a single, isolated response, then an informal discussion might assist the teacher to view her action objectively. This type of assessment is necessary before determining whether letters should be filed in folders with statements from the teacher and principal.

Repeated excessive punishments, or negative and hostile overreaction based on principle or some other rationalization, require counseling, in-service programs, self-examination, peer assistance, review of one's life and goals, assessment of career goals and current position and motivation to improve. The principal must aid teachers who require such assistance, especially if they have secured tenure.

GUIDELINES

1. Thoroughly investigate all complaints to determine validity, half-truths, point of view, and the objectivity of those concerned.
2. Support the professional staff, but be prepared to counsel, supervise, and take disciplinary action with positive follow-up programs if necessary.
3. Communicate with all those involved; caring and concern are central to the solution of any problem where there are two or more points of view.
4. Maintain the best interests of individual students as your first priority.
5. Invite parent *and* student input for consideration in developing the school's regulations on cheating.

6. Discuss and review with the teaching staff the school's regulations on cheating and develop consensus among the faculty regarding the procedures to be followed in arriving at a constructive approach to the problem—an approach that is compatible with the school's philosophy and learning goals.

SITUATION 14

PROBLEM: Making the PTA a Partner

SITUATION: The Faculty Meeting

by
Angela Bruno

The one hundred and ten teachers at Hoover High School were milling around in the spacious conference room. Ten or twelve of them were at the huge coffee makers filling their paper cups; the noisiest group was selecting cookies freshly baked by the junior home economics class.

Mr. Holland, the principal, came into the conference room at 3:00 p.m. sharp, smiling—as was his custom—but instead of stopping, he went straight to the speaker's stand to begin the last regularly scheduled faculty meeting of the year.

The staff was in an unusually receptive mood for the final meeting, perhaps, in part, because of the real assistance that the PTA Committee, chaired by Mrs. Wilhelm, had provided in smoothing out some sticky problems with their student-teacher program.

After the reading and approval of the minutes, and a few preliminary announcements, Mr. Holland opened the discussion by

ENLISTING COMMUNITY COOPERATION 79

simply asking, "I'd like to know how you would like future in-service programs to be scheduled."

Jane Roman, the new business teacher, stood up immediately to be recognized and asked, "Why not schedule all of them the week *before* classes begin?—when everybody's fresh and eager, and—" "Speak for yourself," interrupted Joe Herold. "I say we have minimum days—like Peabody High does—definitely no outside-of-school hours! No way a week early!"

Paul Redman, the History Department chairperson, was obviously disgusted with Joe's remarks, and in his serious, analytical style reasoned, "One of the limitations of our in-service experience, because we *are* such a large faculty, has been the lack of participation. Only a few of us can become actively involved in the presentations. Why not schedule in-service programs during our preparation periods? I think the advantages of small-group discussions are worth giving up a preparation period for now and then."

"Maybe for you!" called one person. "Not on your life!" screamed another. "I need my prep period!" Jan Gardiner shouted. "I need three more prep periods!" an outraged speaker called.

Mr. Holland looked tolerantly amused and then asked if there were any more serious suggestions.

Mrs. Nickels rose to suggest Saturday scheduling, but several teachers objected because they already were registered for Saturday classes. Joe Herold again rose to be recognized, and this time with a little enthusiasm, ventured: "How about that classy Chi-Chi Restaurant? Make it something special—off campus and—" "For certain guest speakers," seconded Miss Roman, "I think that's a very good idea."

Mrs. Paulson was really grumbling to herself; just about everyone heard her say, "I've had it with those guest speakers. They talk a good line, but let them come and teach my remedial English classes!"

Joe Herold rose again, "Mrs. Wilhelm and her PTA committee were more help than any speaker we ever had." The teachers broke into spontaneous applause for Kate Wilhelm who had a very broad smile but had, so far, just listened.

"Maybe we should have an in-service on in-service!" somebody quipped. Then from the back of the room came the question, "Why doesn't that committee continue its good work?"

Mr. Holland looked straight at Mrs. Wilhelm, and she rose to respond to his, "seconding the motion."

"Since my Committee has already wrestled with aspects of this scheduling problem, I would be willing, and I think I speak for the other members of the Committee as well, to work on this problem with those interested teachers, parents and the principal."

The meeting was adjourned at 4:00 p.m.

KEY ISSUES

A. How should a principal involve an entire staff in decisions that concern them?
B. Which tasks are suitable for joint teacher/PTA/principal planning and action?

ANALYSIS

Mr. Holland could have imposed scheduling tailored to his school without a full faculty discussion. He also could have delegated his responsibility entirely to the willing and competent Mrs. Wilhelm and her successful committee. He chose to do neither. Instead, he acted on the understanding that true involvement includes the rational, and sometimes even the not-so-rational, opinions and needs of specific faculty members.

Mr. Holland's ability to conduct an animated, but orderly, faculty meeting and to mobilize—but not exploit—the dedicated was well demonstrated by that active, vocal faculty group.

The teachers, without Mr. Holland listing possibilities, had formulated several scheduling options for *themselves*! Even the tone of the meeting was constructive and not unrealistic; and the appreciation for Mrs. Wilhelm and her PTA committee was sincere and not exploitative.

GUIDELINES

1. The entire faculty should have a voice in designing time patterns and topics for in-service based on individual and school needs.
2. The PTA should be involved in real experiences and projects that are viewed as important and meaningful to all concerned.

SITUATION 15

> PROBLEM: Overcoming Supermarket Griping and Sniping at a New Program
>
> SITUATION: Case Study

by
James R. Campbell and John Swanchak

It was 4:30 p.m. on Friday. Michael Osborn, the Bridgeview Elementary School principal, completed the last of his paperwork, and, while donning his coat, glanced out at a cold, drizzly November day. Over the years, his wife and he had developed a "Thank God It's Friday" ritual, and he looked forward to getting home. When he arrived they'd have wine and cheese and talk about things large and small.

Later that afternoon, while settling into their "Garden Room," Mrs. Osborn inquired: "How goes it at The School of Today, Tomorrow or Whatever?" Mike grinned and wondered why this surge of interest in education. "Because," she replied, "while at the supermarket, I met Mildred Starret who told me that Alice Bingstrom was blowing up a storm at what's going on in that innovative program at your school. She was so loud that other shoppers actually turned to stare at us. It seems to me that Mildred is just as emotionally involved in that program as she claims Alice is!"

Apparently, Mrs. Bingstrom had been angered by the quarterly evaluations received by her son, and at a Parent-Teacher conference with Natalie Price, Peter's fifth grade teacher, had expressed her annoyance and concern. Both had used sharp words, the story went, and Mrs. Bingstrom had left outraged.

The Challenge Program had been designed for gifted elementary and middle school students of the district. As part of the enrichment activities, the program for fifth graders included a multi-age science and mathematics core taught by middle school teachers. From its inception, Mildred Starret had been the spokesperson for parents who opposed the concept. She warned that such programs were perniciously elitist; she questioned the prudence of "special privileges and treatment" for the few—especially at the elementary level; she cautioned that once selected, regardless of performance or personal effort, Challenge students would continue to receive special training because of their purported potential while the diligent, achieving non-gifted would continue to be taught in regular classes. When the Challenge Program was finally approved by the school Board and her own two children were selected, Mrs. Starret reluctantly permitted them to participate. Now, despite the progress of her own youngsters, Mrs. Starret apparently had solicited support from Mrs. Bingstrom.

"What else did Mildred have to say?" Mr. Osborn asked his wife. "Nothing much," she replied, "except that she smiled a lot; it was the type of smile that implies 'I told you so.'"

Mr. Osborn was aware that the Challenge Program had become a status symbol among certain families. Families either revealed pride when their children were "in" or resentment when their children were "out." Since they feared possible repercussions from making it an issue, they essentially remained silent. Those who spoke against the program were usually thought of as being either envious or personally negative.

While not an enthusiastic advocate of the program, Mr. Osborn had supported its implementation. Some of the teachers at the Forest Avenue Elementary School had not. They were worried, they told him, about the effect of institutionally selecting and endorsing selected youngsters for academic preferences and whether the other children were being conditioned to believe that they were inferior.

On Monday Mr. Osborn sent for Mrs. Price. When she arrived, she greeted him cordially and asked what he wanted. He told her that he had heard, inadvertently, about her meeting with Mrs. Bingstrom. "Alice Bingstrom," Mrs. Price said, "has to learn to be objective. She's supposed to be a professional, but she's blind about her son. Peter is basically a nice child who is being pressured to excel by a pushy parent. I told Alice she had ambitions for Peter that were unreal. He tries to please her and live up to what she expects him to be, but he's paying a price for it. He's nervous, anxious and overly conforming. Damn it! It's there to see. He's an 'overachiever,' and year by year it gets harder for him to compete with brighter children. That's why I told her that the best place for Peter is in a regular class where he would be if it wasn't for that elitist Challenge Program."

Alice Bingstrom's family was very successful. One of her brothers was a cancer researcher, another was a surgeon and a younger sister was a college dean. In her early thirties she had married a plumbing contractor who had not attended college. Peter was their only child. Mrs. Bingstrom taught English in the district's high school and was a strict and demanding teacher. From the beginning she had openly let Peter's teachers know when she was displeased with his achievement or progress. She had concluded her talk with Mrs. Price by emphatically stating that she would never consent to Peter's return to a regular classroom and would contest his removal from the program.

Next, Mr. Osborn met with Rebecca Sharp. She was the teacher who developed and supervised out-of-class activities for students in the Challenge Program at the Bridgeview Elementary School. Mrs. Sharp was a bubbly person who reported that she became bored by doing the same old things over and over again. The novel and the new, she said, excited and challenged her.

"The problem with Natalie Price," Mrs. Sharp told the principal, "is that she only feels secure with structure and routine. She's a good teacher, but she refuses to examine the possibilities of providing alternatives to free children from authority and syllabi—to give them a chance to become more than they are and to be creative. Natalie doesn't see any sense in children's acquiring decision-making skills, learning how-to-learn techniques and interpersonal behaviors, because those aren't taught in a conventional way. Sure, Peter and a few others in the program are floundering a bit, but you should have confidence in human potential, and you have to be an open and caring person. This is a process program, and it will take time before its benefits can be demonstrated. In spite of what Natalie thinks, education has to move ahead, not retrogress."

After Mrs. Sharp left, Mr. Osborn called John O'Brien, a middle school teacher who had been a driving force in the design, development and implementation of the Program, and who had become its full-time director. He told John about the Bingstrom incident and suggested they meet with Lydia Johnson and Gene Stinnett, the science and mathematics teachers in the Program. A time was arranged, and, before hanging up, John O'Brien thanked Mr. Osborn for his help in promoting and sustaining the Program.

When the group finally met, the principal outlined Mrs. Price's analysis of Peter Bingstrom. Ms. Johnson, a fourth year teacher, said that although she shared those perceptions, she had to point out that Peter—one of her poorer achievers—seemed to enjoy the class and worked persistently on assignments. She found him eager to please and grateful when praised. Mr. Stinnett disagreed. "I've been at this business a bit longer than Lydia," he noted. "Peter is a slightly above-average student who finds conceptual mathematics difficult and increasingly beyond him. He tries. Oh! How he tries. He's barely surviving through effort, and, I suspect, coaching by his mother. The best thing that could happen to this boy would be to be placed in a regular class where he belongs." Ms. Johnson did not counter those comments; neither did Mr. O'Brien.

Later that day Mr. Osborn talked with Peter. The boy was of average height but was considerably overweight. He was polite, tense and obviously apprehensive. The principal asked him how school was going. Peter, who stuttered in stressful situations, said it was going well, that he liked school and that he was getting a lot out of the Challenge Program. "Are you having any problems?" Mr. Osborn inquired. Peter frowned and replied, "You must mean mathematics. Mr. Stinnett is a very good teacher, but I should be trying harder. I'm not doing as well as I should because I've not been giving math the time it requires, and I'm not concentrating enough. It won't happen again, and I'm sure I'll do better next quarter."

When Peter left, Mr. Osborn asked his secretary to contact Mrs. Bingstrom and ask her to see him. When they met, Mrs. Bingstrom apologized for any inconvenience she might have caused. She reminded him, however, that Peter's future was important to her and that, although she was a teacher, she was also a parent. Mr. Osborn assured her that he was not inconvenienced, that he understood her concern and that he, too, was interested in Peter's welfare.

"I know," she said, "that Peter is not achieving as well as he should and that some non-Program students are achieving at higher levels than some students in the Program. Gifted and non-gifted children, however, do not function equally well in all areas of their lives." She paused, and then continued. "Achievement is largely a result of maturity; the maturity of self-discipline, initiative and motivation. That maturity comes to different people at different times in their lives. Just because a gifted child is not currently achieving well doesn't mean that he should be locked into learning at a rate far below his ability. The potential of a gifted underachiever may be realized only with maturity."

"But," Mr. Osborn suggested, "when making judgments about children, shouldn't we also weigh the impact of cognitive demands upon the child's emotional and social development?"

"If this is leading," Mrs. Bingstrom angrily replied, "to a request for permission to withdraw Peter from the Challenge Program, I will not give it!"

KEY ISSUES

A. What, if anything, should be done about Peter Bingstrom and other youngsters in the Challenge Program who are not performing as well as expected or even as well as some not classified as gifted? Should the principal: (1) ignore the issue; (2) attempt to mollify the protagonists (Mrs. Price and Mrs. Bingstrom); or (3) wait for developments that would either resolve or intensify problems for individual students?

B. Since events seemed to be polarizing the staff, should he: (1) openly and publicly support the Program (and Mr. O'Brien and Mrs. Sharp); (2) oppose the Program (and win the approval of Mrs. Price and many of the faculty of the Bridgeview Elementary School); or (3) suggest that the Program should be modified; and (4) specify how? If he resorted to the latter, would dialogue replace emotion or would it merely exacerbate the situation and, in the end, antagonize everyone?

C. Would recent events arouse the resentfully silent and/or activate the uninvolved? Would that arousal develop community following that could not be ignored?

D. What should be done about Mrs. Price? Could she be expected to continue to quietly endure a program she opposed? Or, given her confrontation with Mrs. Bingstrom, would she, by word and deed, encourage the faculty to challenge the "disruption" of their classes and a program "which was based upon the foggy notions of ivory-towered types who knew nothing about teaching children."

E. Should anything be said to Mrs. Sharp? Would her ebullience, enthusiasm and absolute certainty about the Program's benefits ultimately persuade her colleagues?

F. How should John O'Brien's appeal for support be handled? Should they meet and candidly discuss the involved personalities, the problems of the Challenge Program and a strategy for supporting the Program? Or should the principal remain objective and noncommital?

G. As instructional leader, what plan or set of strategies should Mr. Osborn embrace to determine the continuation, elimination or modification of the Challenge Program?

ANALYSIS

Mr. Osborn spent an evening sifting, sorting and organizing what had happened. The Challenge Program was, and continued to be, controversial. Approximately half the teachers at the Bridgeview Elementary School either had doubts and misgivings or were opposed to it; they had, however, agreed to try the program, and it was being implemented. Mr. Osborn feared that the Peter Bingstrom incident would reawaken latent doubts, give voice to the opposed and rouse the neutral. He also wondered, as many of the teachers did, about giving students with high test scores special treatment. Moreover, Mr. Osborn was uncomfortable about having those students who appeared unable to live up to their expected performance continue in the program. He rejected as specious the argument that they would perform better when they matured; it's difficult for a student to achieve better when he's failing and his self-image suffers.

The Board of Education, however, had mandated the Challenge Program, and Mr. Osborn believed that, whatever his personal concerns, his duty was to support and improve it if he could. Therefore, he wanted to avoid bickering and discord. Clearly then, the issues raised by the Peter Bingstrom incident had to be addressed. Unless they were, they could reduce the commitment of the supportive faculty to the Challenge Program. Mr. Osborn dismissed fleeting thoughts of suggesting immediate modifications; since the Program had just been initiated, such proposals might be precipitous and cause confusion and doubt before the staff had the opportunity to iron out its wrinkles.

Consequently, he decided he would call a faculty meeting and ask that the Challenge Program be given the time it had to have to fulfill its objectives so that, ultimately, it could be fairly and objectively evaluated. After one year of operation, sensible and rational modifications, if they were necessary, could be made.

As for Mildred Starret, Mr. Osborn intended to call John O'Brien, express his concern about her potential as an adversary and volunteer to meet with her. He would try to persuade her that the Challenge Program deserved a chance to succeed or fail on its merits.

Natalie Price, Mr. Osborn realized, would be difficult. He was aware that she was reputed to have said that she would no longer be passive and submit to administrative requests for cooperation. Such statements surprised him since over the years Mrs. Price seemed to indicate that she had confidence in his abilities, his professional judgments and his fairness. If that was true (and he hoped that it was), Mr. Osborn proposed to ask her to work further with the concept and to note objections and constructive suggestions while similtaneously lending her talents and abilities to support the Challenge Program.

Then there was Mrs. Sharp. He planned to tell her that her role was critical in the success or failure of the experiment. She had to be sensitive about her relationships with classroom teachers. For them, Rebecca Sharp *was* the Challenge Program, not merely a teacher who organized and supervised out-of-class activities for students. Unfortunately, others did not have her drive and energy, nor did they share her educational vision or philosophy. In addition, they, too, believed that they had been successful classroom teachers; insinuating that they were not particularly sensitive to the qualities of gifted students would not win them over. Teachers would be impressed by observable results—not words; by progress toward goals—not theories; they would be unmoved by images of what might be. They, too, had to be part of the process and to feel worthwhile and important to the total Program.

Mr. Osborn decided to meet with John O'Brien. He would share his questions and uncertainties about the Challenge Program but would assure him that he would be unequivocally supportive during this year of evaluation. He would outline what he was going to say to Mrs. Price and Mrs. Sharp, and he would propose that Mr. O'Brien, Mrs. Sharp and he meet regularly with the faculty of the school to review what was going well, to discuss aspects of the program that were vague or unclear and to explore adjustments that could or should be made in the continuing pursuit of the Program's objectives. At those sessions he would advise Mr. O'Brien that honesty and candor were vital; if teachers sensed insincerity or condescension, they would assume that they were being manipulated to serve personal, rather than professional, ambitions and the meetings would become exercises in futility.

Finally, there was Peter Bingstrom. His mother was determined that he should achieve academically because she considered it an essential first step toward becoming prominent as an adult and because it reinforced her belief that Peter was a superior child. Consequently, she would fight to obtain what she perceived to be advantages for him. Why she behaved as she did, Mr. Osborn left to psychologists to determine. He could neither make decisions nor conjecture about motivation. He had to deal with the negative consequences of her posture. Mrs. Bingstrom was convinced that Peter was gifted, and the opinions and evaluations of teachers would not alter that. She did not want Peter dropped from the Challenge Program (and, probably, neither did Mr. O'Brien and Mrs. Sharp).

He decided to request the Challenge teachers and coordinators to establish assistance programs in areas of current difficulty for any students who were initially screened and accepted as gifted students. They were to record achievement, interests, learning preferences, modality strengths, motivation, evidence of self-image and samples of work at their level. Criteria for admission and the objectives for Challenge were to be measured against the performance of all concerned. Students who initially were admitted to the Program would be permitted to stay for one year unless teachers and parents both opted for transfer. The specifics of those evaluation procedures would be decided by a steering committee of Challenge staff, classroom teachers, parents and the principal.

GUIDELINES

1. Recognize that any new program is likely to draw strong advocates, neutrals and antagonists from staff, administration and community.
2. Focus on positive objectives and outcomes; deal firmly and fairly with emotional responses.

3. Timing, as in so many aspects of administration, is critical. Avoid premature introduction or withdrawal of programs; build substantial support and commitment to pilot projects or mandated programs.
4. Take action during a building crisis. Establish representative committees, evaluation teams or planning groups. Delegate both responsibility and authority to accomplish goals. Remain in charge and in control as you evaluate each phase of their responsibilities with them.

Supervising Assistant Principals

SITUATION 16

> **PROBLEM:** Linking the Chain of Command Within a Building
>
> **SITUATION:** Teachers' Room Ultimatum

by
Virginia L. Kavanagh

It's a Friday afternoon, the students have been dismissed, and the staff is not free to leave the building for another fifteen minutes. Ray Frank, the building's Union Representative, stops Jim Watson, the assistant principal.

"Jim, do you have a couple of minutes? I'd like to talk to you. A few of the teachers are planning to meet this afternoon, and we wondered if you'd join us."

"What's up, Ray?"

"It's a matter that has a lot of the teachers uptight, and we thought if we could discuss it with you, you might be able to help us handle the situation."

Jim joins Ray and several other teachers in the faculty room. The building is relatively empty except for this group and the principal who is finishing some work in his office. As Ray and Jim enter the faculty room, Jim is welcomed by the staff who appear pleased with his presence. It seems that George Watson, a teacher on staff for eighteen years, in his middle forties and popular with the students, has been having a particularly rough year. As far as the principal is concerned, George is a teacher who comes to school late with considerable regularity, has had a spotty attendance record this year, has been seen and heard "exploding" at students, has not stayed for faculty meetings and, in general, appears rather harried. The teachers express their concern about George and their antagonism for the principal who they feel is "out to get" him. Apparently, the principal has had George into his office to discuss all of this, and George views that as harassment. He has complained bitterly to other teachers who are very sympathetic to his cause since they know that he has been going through a very difficult time at home. His oldest son, age fifteen, has been involved in a very serious drug problem. That concern has generated many home problems, including a deteriorating marriage; George and his wife are talking about divorce.

The teachers believe that all of these factors should be considered. They tell the assistant principal, "Get him (the principal) off George's back. If you don't, we will go to the Union and grieve, charging him with harassment."

The assistant principal asks, "Did Bill know all this was happening at home with George?"

"No, we don't think so."

"Why didn't somebody tell him? Maybe he'd understand the situation and know how to handle it a little better."

"Because the man has no heart," the teachers respond. "He doesn't really care. All he wants to do is run a tight ship. If that means getting rid of George, that's what he's going to do."

Jim asks, "How do you know that? Has anybody gone to speak with Bill (the principal)?"

"We told you, we can't talk to him. He has no heart! Look, we invited you in to tell you to get him off George's back. Otherwise, we're going to file a grievance, and Bill's going to be in big trouble."

Jim asks the group, "What exactly do you want me to do? You said to get Bill off George's back. What are you suggesting?"

The teachers reply, "Tell him. Tell him to lay off. Tell him we're going to the Union."

"Why don't you tell that to Bill yourselves? Why come to me?"

"Because we thought you'd be able to understand it. There's no point in our talking to him."

The meeting ends rather abruptly as Bill walks into the faculty room for a final cup of coffee before going home. The conversation changes, people leave fairly rapidly, and when everyone has gone, Bill asks Jim, "What was that all about?"

KEY ISSUES

A. Did the faculty want Jim to use his judgment in handling a difficult situation?

B. How should Jim respond to Bill's question?
C. Was Jim right in participating in the meeting?
D. Did the teachers have a valid point?
E. Is it appropriate for Jim to act as a buffer between the faculty and the principal?
F. To whom does Jim owe his loyalty—the faculty or the principal?
G. If Jim doesn't line up with the staff, will he lose his effectiveness in future dealings?
H. As an administrator, does Jim have to represent the principal's point of view?
I. Do situations like this one include more than one "right side"? What makes it complex and not just either/or?

ANALYSIS

The teachers obviously were expressing a very real concern for one of their colleagues. Furthermore, they had determined the course of action they thought was appropriate. That is, that George be permitted to continue his pattern of behavior without interference from the principal. We have no evidence that the faculty really wanted Jim to exercise his judgment as to how the matter should be resolved. In fact, they presented the assistant principal with an ultimatum. "Get the principal off George's back, or we grieve."

As a wise administrator, Jim must realize that he has other alternatives. As a caring person, Jim wants exactly what the faculty wants—help for George. Considering the situation, Jim should give himself time to think through what happened and not rush to make a quick reply. Therefore, when Bill asked the question, "What was that all about?" Jim might grant himself the weekend for reflective thought, if needed. He might reply truthfully that he wants to sort out what was said and that he'd see Bill first thing Monday morning.

Jim should consider certain questions, such as, what were the teachers really telling him?—they seemed to be saying that they were worried about George. Once he realizes that this was the real focus of the meeting, he will be free to exercise options rather than merely respond to the ultimatum. The group is upset, and George obviously needs help. Jim must now wrestle with the question of whether or not Bill is capable of understanding the personal problems affecting George. The teachers' attitudes might lead us to believe that there is something in Bill's makeup that makes this kind of confidence difficult, if not impossible. Nevertheless, the fact remains that if the situation is to be dealt with, there is a chain of command to be observed. Bill *is* George's superior; he is involved in George's evaluation, and if he is to make an informed judgment, he needs information. Jim might choose to discuss the background information with Bill and take the point of view that George is a person in need of help; one who needs to be dealt with compassionately as well as professionally.

Jim has another option of returning to the group and suggesting that either its members speak with Bill, or delegate him to do so; not to deliver ultimatums but to enlist his aid in helping George. Further, he might suggest to George that he do so himself. At any rate, it is critical that the principal operate with full awareness of the circumstances.

The question of divided loyalties should not be an issue here. In fact, Jim's responsibility as assistant principal is to maximize faculty participation in the educational process. Therefore, whatever is done to help George as an individual will aid the group which is feeling the stress of the situation and the principal whose responsibility it is to maintain a competent staff. The faculty and administrator in this situation are *not* opposing entities.

Jim now has the unique opportunity of drawing principal and staff closer together. Whatever Jim can do to help the staff understand the administrative responsibilities that are involved, and whatever he can do to help the administrator understand faculty concerns, is a challenge to his ability as an administrator who may one day become a principal.

Certainly, Jim has an obligation to help both the staff and the administration understand each other's point of view. He is not there merely to represent the administration's viewpoint. It is precisely his role to combine faculty and administration as partners in the solution of a critical problem.

Because Jim is a good administrator, he should be pleased that the faculty recognizes that he is approachable. It is to be hoped that he can draw both the faculty and administrator into a closer relationship.

Jim's problem is essentially one of helping staff members to understand the relationship between themselves and the administration and helping the administration to understand that it exists to make the work of the faculty most productive for students. Therefore, someone, be it Jim, the faculty, or George himself, must talk with Bill, and Bill must understand that George is functioning in a new pattern and that considerations should be extended but that he must be assisted toward a rapid rehabilitation. If Jim is successful in defusing the situation and helping all to understand that a punitive approach is inappropriate, but that students' needs must take first priority, he will have served all parties well.

Jim was pleased at the rapidity with which these thoughts had passed through his mind. His frown disappeared, and he smiled at Bill who then seemed to relax a bit. Jim felt he had built sufficient trust with Bill to review the situation that afternoon. "Bill, I'd like to buy you a cup of coffee down at the diner. There are a couple of things I need your help with, and I'd like to talk to you about them in a relaxed atmosphere."

Jim smiled again. He knew he was doing the right thing. To wait until Monday would have raised Bill's concern about the "meeting" he had interrupted. Moreoever, Jim had accepted the responsibility thrust upon him and had neither returned it to the complaining group nor to George, the involved teacher.

He was growing as an administrator, and he trusted Bill to recognize that growth. He and Bill walked toward his car. He felt good.

GUIDELINES

1. Listen to all complaints, requests and suggestions.
2. Remain objective.
3. Analyze situations to determine the heart of the issue, the essence of the problem or the real cause of a complaint.
5. Act responsibly to bring all parties toward an understanding of their common goals.

SITUATION 17

> PROBLEM: Evaluating the Instructional Effectiveness of the Assistant Principal
>
> SITUATION: Taking Charge—Directly

by
Rita Dunn and Kenneth Dunn

Mark Spreadson was the principal of three small, rural elementary schools and was responsible for improving instruction in all three. Each had an assistant principal who was in charge and who had been given authority and responsibility for all aspects of instruction.

Mark spent most of his time in two of the buildings for the first three years of his tenure as principal because he felt he had to work closely with those two assistants on school climate, curriculum direction, and initial stages of training teachers to understand and apply the latest knowledge of teaching and learning.

The third building, known as the Beach School, had a young assistant principal who was hired because of her knowledge of and enthusiasm for individualized instruction the year before Mark arrived. Now in his fourth year, and satisfied with the progress in the first two buildings, Mark began to spend the major portion of his time in the Beach School.

Barbara Whitney, the assistant principal, had transferred from a low socioeconomic district in a large midwestern city. She provided demonstration lessons and in-service sessions for those members of the faculty who were interested. As a result, some movement toward individualization had occurred.

Mark entered the school one morning in late September and was greeted by a "task force" of sixth grade students who had been assigned to guide him to the first Discussion Area. There, he joined Ms. Whitney and two teachers who had volunteered to share their coffee break with Mark to explain the school's emerging program.

The teachers explained that only six of the current twelve-member faculty had begun individualizing. The remaining teachers had been experimenting with some of the new techniques but had elected to go slowly and to see how the others fared. Parents had been involved in the training process and were assisting the six teachers by preparing stencils and dittos, correcting papers when requested, reading textbook passages into tape recorders to assist children who had difficulty learning to read or who read poorly, working with below-level youngsters to reinforce concepts and information, and helping to supervise students as they operated equipment and media.

All of the six teachers had introduced several small-group techniques to their classes so that youngsters might begin to work independently without constant teacher guidance and supervision. They admitted that these techniques worked well with many youngsters, but that some students appeared to be resistant to functioning without continual direction. For those, the parent aides had been assigned to persuade, encourage and help them through the learning process.

Mark then walked through the building to view those classrooms in which the six teachers had begun to individualize.

Another team of students guided him to the first room. They politely explained that, beyond that point, the building tour was self-explanatory. Before the students left, he asked, "How do you like individualization?" The youngsters laughed, shrugged their shoulders, and said, "It's all right!" They giggled and went to their own classes.

He entered the first room. It was arranged differently from any he had ever seen. There were only ten or twelve desks in the room, but there were many "instructional areas" and chairs for the thirty youngsters he had counted. A lounge sofa was used as a room divider toward the far right and several carpeted areas extended into corners and nooks where students were crouched over books, charts, media and other instructional materials. Tables appeared to form a nucleus of learning areas and large, well-printed signs announced: Mathematics Learning Station, Media Corner, Game Table, Little Theater, Interest Center and Magic Carpet. The room appeared to be a hub of activity as children interacted freely, but quietly, moving from area to area with purpose and at their option.

He walked to the section called Interest Center and noted the multitude of reading materials on varied levels. Three or four pupils worked together to achieve the objectives listed for them on their contracts, but each of the students was using a different text.

Mark inspected the Game Table where some students were creating a game about the life of Benjamin Franklin, and others were doing a crossword puzzle on George Washington. At the Media Corner two boys were beginning to project the filmstrip they had just completed on John Paul Jones.

Along the side of the bookcases were several different dittos labeled "Circle of Knowledge," "Team Learning," "Case Study," and "Simulations." Mark asked a few of the students what those were, and they told him that they were ways for the students to learn more about the heroes they had been studying. He picked up the ditto called "Team Learning" and noted that the question on it was: "Name as many American Heroines as you can in three minutes." The ditto on simulations had several paragraphs describing the way Molly Pitcher demonstrated bravery when her husband was killed at his post and was followed by two kinds of questions. Somewhere in the material the answers could be found to the first type of question. The youngsters had to think through answers to the other type of question according to their opinions, the persuasive arguments of others, the insights they gained, etc. This was sometimes done through "roles" that the youngsters played based on descriptions of the parts they had selected for the simulation.

The walls were attractively covered with commercially produced charts that described the economic bases for revolution. Mark wondered why they were displayed and asked a pupil whether this was an area of study for the class. The child responded that the chart was part of the next unit that the class would be studying and that the teacher was trying to arouse the group's interest and curiosity in the topic by exposing the children to the display.

In the second room Mark visited, he noticed that while some small groups were busily involved in mathematics games and assignments, others were reading with the teacher, individuals were working on science experiments, and still others appeared to be tutoring each other. The chalkboard had a series of assignments on it in each of the four major curriculum areas and also listed several alternatives in the creative arts. When questioned about this procedure, some of the students explained that they had required work that had to be done but that they could complete the exercises anytime at all within a two-day period. "What happens to the students who don't complete their work?" He asked. "They can't learn as much!" the students quickly replied.

In walking around the room, the principal noticed that although children were engaged in different activities, those who were involved in the same curriculum area were using identical materials; the same basal reader, the same social studies text on the same page, the same science experiments and the same mathematics exercises. The tapes that were available also appeared to be on the same topic and at one level.

The teacher was so engrossed in individual discussions with pupils that she did not have time to speak with Mark, only to nod politely. While she was talking to students, six other children appeared to be vying for her attention. The youngsters around her waited, often impatiently, to receive answers to their questions.

He noted that the morning had flown by quickly and that it was time for lunch. Mark left the class and was walking toward the assistant principal's office when he realized that groups of youngsters were walking unescorted through the halls to the cafeteria. They were talking zealously, but without much noise. One or two did run, but they were quickly blocked by slower-moving children who would not be pushed aside. The runners slowed down and altered their pace. He wondered where the teachers of these pupils were and whether the students were permitted to walk to their lunch area without an escort.

Mark then noticed a teacher walking with nine pupils in the same general direction. Looking at the nine, he guessed that they were probably nonconformists. One placed a hand on the boy in front of him and pushed surreptitiously. Another tripped a child passing alongside, while a third snatched the hat off the head of a girl directly in front. The teacher with the nine walked slowly, keeping each of the children within close range. As they began to misbehave, she stopped, rearranged the group, reprimanded the instigators, and then walked on with them.

Mark began to reflect on what he had seen that morning. He wondered which behavioral patterns were associated directly with the concept of "individualization" and which were not necessarily designed to promote individual student growth.

KEY ISSUES

    A. What criteria should a principal establish for the improvement of teaching and learning?
    B. How can a principal aid his assistants in implementing and evaluating instructional programs?
    C. Which observational listings can be used to evaluate teaching and learning?

ANALYSIS

Mark Spreadson was generally pleased with what he had seen but knew he had made the right choice in electing to spend more time at the Beach School.

He scheduled a series of meetings with the assistant principal and then with the entire faculty.

After establishing criteria and goals for individualizing instruction, Mark and Ms. Whitney met with the six who had begun to individualize and assisted them directly in the classroom.

Next, he designed faculty meetings to provide insights into effective instruction for the entire staff. The six who still used only traditional approaches were invited to participate in a total self-evaluation of the school.

After the following charts were developed, all twelve teachers agreed to attend in-service sessions and move toward total individualization at a pace comfortable for each.

A. Positive Observations

Appropriate Student Behaviors	Appropriate Adult Behaviors	Appropriate Behavioral Outcomes
1. Students were serving as guides for visitors.	1. The administrator provided in-service sessions and demonstration lessons for interested faculty	1. The administrator provided leadership toward instructional improvement.

Appropriate Student Behaviors	Appropriate Adult Behaviors	Appropriate Behavioral Outcomes
2. Students worked toward completion of their objectives ...	2. Teachers volunteered to acquaint visitors with their program.	2. Teachers were permitted to volunteer to individualize and, therefore, were treated as individuals by the administrator.
3. ... through their own learning style.	3. Parent volunteers assisted teachers.	3. The program was described as "emerging" and teachers were permitted to move toward individualization at their own pace.
4. Students used multilevel and varied instructional resources in room #1.	4. Teachers used small group techniques (the first step toward individualization).	4. Room #1 was divided into instructional areas.
5. Students created resources and used them.	5. Parent aides worked directly with students who required adult assistance.	5. Parent involvement permitted more effective use of teacher time.
6. Students in room #2 were permitted to schedule their own activities.	6. Teachers escorted those youngsters who had not demonstrated the ability to conduct themselves responsibly without supervision.	6. Parent volunteers had been trained.
7. Students were permitted to walk through the halls without direct supervision and most did so politely.	7. Teachers disciplined students when necessary.	7. Walls were attractively covered, to "arouse group interest and curiosity."

Appropriate Student Behaviors	Appropriate Adult Behaviors	Appropriate Behavioral Outcomes
8. Students were actively involved in their own learning.	8. Teachers permitted self-pacing and self-selection of sociological pairs and groups.	8. Varied materials and multimedia resources were evident in both rooms.
9. Unescorted students who ran through the corridors were blocked properly by other children.	9. An attempt was made to ask high-level questions about Molly Pitcher.	9. Individualizing techniques included student latitude on time, method, and order of completing assignments.
10. Children worked well together (perfecting multimedia or actually developing filmstrips).	10. Aides worked with those who learned more slowly.	10. An active but not frenetic classroom with self-directed learning was observed.
11. Children learned from each other. (When a person teaches, he learns from the experience.)		11. Dittoed questions went beyond the detailed factual materials ordinarily used.
12. Self-discipline was practiced.		12. Wall displays were used to stimulate learning.
13. Peer discipline was apparent.		
14. Children worked on a project together but used different texts.		
15. Small groups were active and involved in varied techniques.		
16. Children interacted in small groups through peer sharing.		

B. Areas that Require Improvement

Inappropriate Student Behaviors	Inappropriate Adult Behaviors	Inappropriate Behavioral Outcomes
1. Students should not have developed a filmstrip at the game table. (Instructional areas should be correctly used to facilitate student progress.)	1. Parents assisted only the six teachers involved in individualizing, rather than all.	1. In-service training is completely optional. Faculty should be exposed to techniques and then permitted to gradually adapt or discard them. Some teachers waiting to see "How others fare" may have been rationalizing their inactivity.
2. Students in room #2 had single-level resources only and even these were limited in number.	2. The assistant principal seemed enthusiastic about individualization, but did not correct the apparent inconsistencies in the program; e.g., incorrectly established instructional areas, single-level resources in room #2, etc.	2. Most teachers had not begun to individualize instruction.
3. Basal readers should not be used in an individualized reading program.	3. Parent aides were asked to help students who did not learn in groups. (Not all children can learn in groups.)	3. Room #1 had language arts Learning Station resources (multi-level, single curriculum materials) inappropriately placed at an "Interest Center" (which should house inter-disciplinary resources).

Inappropriate Student Behaviors	Inappropriate Adult Behaviors	Inappropriate Behavioral Outcomes
4. Children giggled and shrugged inarticulately when asked about individualization. Children needed to know more about individulaization to explain the concept rather than merely to guide visitors to physical facilities.	4. Parents worked only with below-level students.	4. Some specialized areas were not well-utilized for their own unique purposes.
5. Room #2 was not individualized. Everyone involved in the same curriculum was using identical materials at the same time.	5. Children who did not complete work were not necessarily helped, nor was the work modified for them.	5. The dittoed "team learning" was a circle of knowledge; the simulation was a team learning that utilized role playing. The small-group instructional techniques were being incorrectly used.
6. Children had no involvement in the selection of topics of study.	6. Children's materials were not posted to give recognition, to encourage creativity, and to evaluate progress.	6. Commercially produced wall charts were used. These are not as desirable as those that are student-designed.
7. Children tried to get the teacher's attention in room # 2 without a set system. They were impatient and wasting time. (The teacher's role should be shared with other adults and students as resource people.)	7. Parents appeared to be disciplining and repeating instead of finding new ways of approaching the students.	7. Representative materials should have related directly to current (and not future) studies.

Inappropriate Student Behaviors	Inappropriate Adult Behaviors	Inappropriate Behavioral Outcomes
8. The children appeared to be involved in essentially cognitive learning. No attempt was made to develop the student's affective or psycho-motor characteristics. (To be whole people, we need more than cognitive learning. There is little evident expression of feeling indicated in either room.)	8. Teacher efforts were directed toward cognitive learning only.	8. The teacher should have taught her students to continue work in an area where they could progress independently while waiting for her assistance. No system had been established for obtaining help when necessary.
	9. There were no teacher diagnoses of a child's inability to complete work.	9. Specific individualization techniques are an important part of training teachers; these were not apparent.
	10. Quality and quantity of assignments were not reassessed by teachers.	10. Team learning should be used to introduce new material, not for reinforcement as was the case here.
	11. There was no evidence of evaluation (which is an integral part of the learning process) in either room.	
	12. There was no indication in room #1 that children had any exposure	

Inappropriate Student Behaviors	Inappropriate Adult Behaviors	Inappropriate Behavioral Outcomes
	to science. Although there was a mathematics Learning Station indicated, there is no mention of anything being studied except social studies in terms of the American Revolution. (Science and Math could well be integrated into this topic.)	

GUIDELINES

1. Specific behavioral outcomes designed to measure appropriate results in terms of staff and student performance should be designed by the principal and the staff.
2. Principals must spend considerable time in classrooms observing, evaluating, and suggesting strategies to improve teaching and learning.
3. Observations, peer evaluation, in-service meetings and series should be planned to devise assessment of appropriate student behaviors, teacher behaviors and behavioral outcomes. Sharing by teachers and administrators promotes improvement and motivation.

SITUATION 18

> PROBLEM: Working on Desegregation Problems
>
> SITUATION: Cafeteria Observations

by
Shirley A. Griggs

Sheila Hutchins, a young, able, black principal in a middle school that was seventy percent white, twenty-five percent black and five percent "other" minorities, walked through the cafeteria with her assistant principal of two-and-a-half years, Jeff Seiden. They were both extremely concerned. Although they and their staff had diligently worked on school climate and human relations for two full years, they observed only white students talking to whites, blacks clustered together in their usual corners and a small group of isolated Spanish-speaking youngsters seated together.

The young administrator wasn't happy about other manifestations of segregation such as classrooms based on ability that seemed to separate racial and ethnic groups, similarly segregated cocurricular clubs, and "educational" practices that only served to impede the integration process.

Sheila and Jeff had met with student leaders of all groups, interested and active parents, guidance counselors and respected veteran teachers.

It became clear that the building staff would have to take a new look at their own attitudes, procedures, policies and teaching styles; the old methods simply weren't effective in dealing with today's social problems. Moreover, the students and some of the teachers had identified the behavior patterns and attitudes that they be-

SUPERVISING ASSISTANT PRINCIPALS

lieved fostered a negative atmosphere for learning in their school. For example:

1. Apparent low expectations for the academic performance of minority youth;
2. Inappropriate instructional materials;
3. Poor interpersonal relationships between selected teachers and certain minority students;
4. Failure to value the contributions of minority children;
5. Grouping some children for instruction on the basis of factors unrelated to their abilities, interests or learning styles;
6. Apparently biased counseling practices of teachers, guidance counselors, and administrators regarding career opportunities and post-secondary education for minority youth;
7. Biased institutional practices resulting in continuous majority student leadership;
8. Failure to relate to minority students as individuals;
9. Purported bias in the administration of discipline; and
10. Lack of openness with students, such as failing to discuss incidents with racial overtones.

KEY ISSUES

A. What are the conditions that would promote genuine in-school integration and quality education for all, regardless of background?
B. How can classroom practices be modified through changes in teachers' and administrators' attitudes?
C. Which program elements are essential to improved desegregation practices?

ANALYSIS AND SOLUTIONS

Jeff Seiden decided to do some reading on the topic. He found a helpful beginning checklist in a book by Pettigrew.[1]

---

[1] Pettigrew, Thomas F., *Prejudice and Pride*, Washington, D.C.: The National Academy of Education (1979).

1. Equal access to the school's resources;
2. Cultural fairness;
3. Classroom—not just school—desegregation;
4. Avoidance of strict "test-score grouping";
5. Maintenance and improvement of services;
6. Initiation of desegregation in the early grades;
7. Consistent school feeder patterns that keep desegregated classes together;
8. Interethnic staff;
9. Substantial, rather than token, minority student percentages; and
10. Minimal confounding of race and socioeconomic class.

He brought these suggested items to his original Study Committee. It decided to discuss the list in light of what had been attempted by the school during the past three years. Those actions included:

1. Focused discussions at faculty meetings;
2. Continued planning sessions during the summer;
3. Several workshops in human relations for the staff;
4. Introduction of a minority history course;
5. Purchase of multiethnic text materials;
6. The establishment of a multiethnic student advisory committee; and
7. A series of human relations field trips.

These were the usual approaches—and apparently they didn't work.

"How could they," Jeff reasoned with a sudden burst of insight. "Not one of them, not even the overnight field trip, was designed to have students *working with each other* on real classroom and school problems!"

Sheila Hutchins joined in. "Jeff's right. We've been blinded by our own traditional approaches to school problems. Students have to cross the line of separation and prejudice on their own by learning, working and playing together. Friendships grow out of peer interaction, common causes, and joint successes. We haven't even done very much to encourage minority students to try out for our teams!"

Now it was Sheila's turn to review the literature. She and the guidance counselors liked the approach suggested by Parker[2] and presented it to the Committee.

It was designed so that black and white student leaders could volunteer to go through the program first to serve as models for the rest of the student body. Initially, ten students would be selected for group counseling with equal numbers from the various ethnic/racial groups represented in the school population. A school counselor would conduct seven sessions of forty-five minutes each, focusing on the following theme areas:

1. *Communication Training.* Group members identify effective and ineffective communication techniques and are placed in pairs to concentrate on listening and speaking effectively to each other.
2. *Communication in Action.* Participants are racially segregated and asked to identify things people of the other race do to hinder effective communication between the races. Those reports then are shared in the larger group; the issues of prejudice, stereotyping and values are discussed.
3. *Attitudes and Feelings.* This session helps members become aware of their personal attitudes and feelings toward other races by discussing their past and present experiences with people of other races.
4. *Awareness of Racial Stereotypes.* This session helps participants become more aware of the stereotypes they hold regarding other races through role-playing the "black militant," "cracker," "slant-eye," "cool black," "wetback" and so on.
5. *Integration Through Recreation.* This activity provides opportunity for interracial contact by participation in segregated and then integrated volleyball teams, followed by discussion of their personal feelings and observations.
6. *Action Plan.* Racially integrated pairs develop a plan for bringing about better relations between black and white students.

---

[2]Parker, Woodrow H., "A Race Relations Program to Improve Integration in High Schools", *The School Counselor* 27 (1979): 119-125.

7. *Follow-up to Action Plan.* During the final session, participants are asked to share the outcomes of their specific action plans.

• • • • • • • • • • • •

Then a student member of the committee spoke out, "You know we tried some of that stuff in those Human Relations meetings you made us go to. We should be here to do more than play roles! Maybe we *do* have to learn how to communicate and all that jazz, but we *know* we need Jo-Boy and the Scraper on our basketball team; you don't have to communicate *that* to us! And I *know* I need help in math from some kid, or I'll never get out of this school 'cause I *don't* understand it from my teacher! We don't need to talk about how we can learn from each other; we just don't know how to get the ball rolling!"

The adults turned in amazement. That was the longest speech by little Marvin Bins that anyone had ever heard. It turned them all toward designing opportunities, experiences, clinics, classes, peer-help groups and other strategies for student interaction across all background lines.

GUIDELINES

1. Evaluate procedures and programs that don't work and isolate those strategies and procedures which should be eliminated from future planning and problem-solving.
2. Review the literature and recent studies to identify those concepts and techniques that offer potential for success.
3. Involve key representatives of all groups concerned; select students, faculty and administrators who care, who have ability and who are committed to improvement.
4. Design workshops that focus on awareness and improved communication, but move quickly into *doing* rather than discussing.
5. Provide real situations for student interaction, problem-solving, peer assistance, learning, goal-setting and teaming in sports, other co-curricular areas *and* academics.

SITUATION 19

> **Problem:** Listening to Students with a Fair, Consistent Ear
>
> **SITUATION:** Emotional Student Appeal

by
Carole A. Decker

The student yearbook editor came tearing into Ms. Warren's homeroom, flushed and angry. "It isn't fair. It just isn't fair!"

"What's wrong, Chris?" asked Ms. Warren, who was the school's yearbook advisor.

"Ms. Belson, the assistant principal, just told us that we can no longer have our special yearbook homeroom," blurted Chris. "She says we have to be mixed in with the other regular homerooms from now on!"

"Why?" asked the startled teacher, who was hearing the news for the first time.

"She said we've all been abusing the privilege," the agitated student replied.

"Well, we'll look into this. Calm down. I'll talk to Ms. Belson and see what's behind it. She's usually fair in her decisions so there must be some good reason for it," said Ms. Warren.

"If we can't have our own homeroom, there's no use trying to put out a yearbook!" Chris was near hysteria. "If that's what she wants, fine! Let *her* make the yearbook. We'll all go on strike! Let's see how she likes that!"

"Take it easy, Chris," Ms. Warren soothed. "It'll work out once we know why it's happening. I'm sure Ms. Belson understands the importance of a yearbook and the work it takes to create one. We'll work it out...somehow."

"I sure hope you can." Chris was calming herself. "It's the only way we can manage our staff and really work as a group. It makes the job of raising funds and accounting for the money easier, because we get to see all the people involved every single day! You've got to explain that to the assistant principal," implored Chris.

"Yes, I agree that the yearbook homeroom is a necessity if we want a quality yearbook," replied Ms. Warren evenly. "I'll see her today as soon as I can."

During her preparation period later that day, Ms. Warren walked down to the school's office to see the assistant principal. She asked Ms. Belson if it was true that the yearbook homeroom was to be discontinued, and if so, why? Ms. Belson appeared annoyed and offered a twofold reason: (1) She felt that the students in the special homerooms (Student Council and yearbook) were merely using the time for social purposes and were "floating about the school building increasing the difficulties of the teachers assigned to hall duty"; and (2) a few teachers had complained to her that it was impossible to keep accurate attendance records because the special homeroom students were listed out of alphabetical sequence, thus requiring a full search of the absentee sheets in order to locate specific names. Ms. Belson said that greater teacher harmony and tighter record keeping would be promoted by her new directive, and after many years of being in charge of co-curricular activities, she knew her decision was correct.

As they discussed the situation further, another reason for dissolving the special homerooms became evident. Ms. Belson conceded that it was primarily the Student Council homeroom that had abused what she called their special privilege. In that case, the Student Council teacher-advisor was often late and even absent from homeroom. That advisor's interest had waned. Correct attendance was seldom taken and reported there, and, as a consequence, the students in that special homeroom had become lax in their self-discipline. Some of the school's teachers had complained about the "privileged few." Ms. Warren argued that that was not sufficient reason to discipline and punish the yearbook staff. Reluctantly, though resolutely, the assistant principal agreed that it might seem unfair to the yearbook students to penalize both special homerooms for the misconduct of one. She insisted that, given the circumstances, the only administratively fair and equitable approach for her to take was to avoid granting a privilege to one group and not the other. She remained firm in her decision to cancel both special homerooms immediately for at least the next school year.

KEY ISSUES

Central to the problem presented here is that students were *not* being dealt with in an administratively fair and equitable manner. If the situation was perceived as one of discriminatory student "elitism" that caused faculty friction, then that particular emotion should have been addressed. On the other hand, if the situation was one of a particular teacher's failure, students should not have been held responsible; especially not students who were not involved in the negative situation. Further, the affected students had not really been made aware of the problem for which they were to serve as the solution. They were labeled as the *cause* of the difficulty and precluded from correcting it themselves. A more reasoned administrative approach would have encouraged the affected students to participate in resolving the difficulties created by their own extracurricular activities. Unilateral administrative fiats often toss the baby out with the bathwater, thus precipitating even greater disregard for, and unhappiness with, inequitable school rules or unnecessarily restrictive regulations.

An administrative policy of handling problems which conveys to students that they, too, are permitted some input to policymaking, encourages student growth and self-discipline. When trusted to supply alternatives, propose solutions and even to implement policy, students readily accept the challenge of being held accountable. Such an approach promotes positive student attitudes, permits the principal and assistant principal to operate in a democratic climate, and often satisfies a staff that is unhappy. Best of all, it creates an open atmosphere of trust, free expression and cooperation within the school.

Such an approach, in this case, would result in the yearbook students working more diligently to create a superlative publication. The Student Council members would strive for greater self-discipline because they would understand that the school's administration was really interested in them and their efforts.

ANALYSIS

The following day Ms. Warren reluctantly relayed the assistant principal's decision to her yearbook staff. All expressed unhappiness and frustration. They vigorously protested that it was not they who had abused a privilege and that it was even more unfair for future yearbook staffs and for future Student Councils to be penalized because of other students' previous misconduct. "Why should we suffer because Student Council was out of line?" they asked. "And why should *next* year's yearbook staff have to work under tighter controls?" They asked if they could, as a group, see Ms. Belson and argue their cause.

Ms. Warren, having read all the appropriate administrative theory texts, said, "Of course. You have a right to voice your opinions and dissatisfactions; and you should." She discussed with the group how best to present their position and how to offer their own solutions. The student staff voted to go en masse to make their appeal. They arranged an appointment with the assistant principal for the next day. Then, with Ms. Warren's guidance, they polished their arguments and suggestions and decided upon a single spokesperson.

At the appointed time, the students appeared before Ms. Belson and presented their point of view and their reasons for wanting to continue as a special homeroom. Ms. Belson, being a clever and wise woman, and remembering that she, too, had once read an administrative theory text, said she would reconsider her decision if the yearbook students could help her solve the problem. She suggested that they establish written guidelines for policing themselves and their peers' conduct and attendance in the special homerooms—rules to which all those students must subscribe. The youngsters readily agreed to the solution and immediately drafted a stringent "Code of Conduct for Special Homeroom Students."

Later, speaking alone with Ms. Warren, the assistant principal abashedly admitted that the advisor had struck at her "Achilles' heel." Guiding students to her with well thought-out arguments and alternative solutions was a cogently creative way to effect change in administrative decisions and existing school policy. She thanked Ms. Warren for her considerate guidance and instruction.

She also imposed upon Ms. Warren, at the opening of the new school year, the obligation of explaining to the school's entire teaching staff the very real function of the special homerooms in order to clarify their need and their utility. Ms. Belson then designated Ms. Warren and a newly appointed Student Council advisor as insurers against their students' abuse of the privilege of special homerooms, thereby establishing a greater teacher responsibility while, simultaneously, affording advisors and students continuation of the desired system.

SUPERVISING ASSISTANT PRINCIPALS

GUIDELINES

1. One group of students should not be penalized for the misconduct of another group.
2. Students should be allowed to participate in resolving problems in which they are involved directly.
3. Students, particularly those involved in extracurricular activities at the secondary level, should be consulted before existing school policy governing their activities is altered. That consultation should result in some responsibility for supervising themselves in their voluntary activities.
4. The disbanding of clubs, special homerooms and extracurricular activities should be researched thoroughly and explored before administrative action is initiated.
5. Administrators should consult regularly with their staffs on issues, procedures and changes. (One never knows when a teacher might have something useful to suggest.)

Situation 20

PROBLEM: Delegating Higher Order Tasks—Sources of Outside Funding

SITUATION: Memos, Meetings and Reports

---

by
Shirley A. Griggs

The Principal of Jefferson High School received the following memorandum from the Coordinator of Funding in the District Office:

> MEMORANDUM
>
> TO: Theodore Smith, Principal, Jefferson High School
> FROM: Pauline Moore, District Coordinator of Funding Projects
> DATE: August 15
> SUBJECT: Termination of Funding in Selected Areas
>
> For the coming academic year, we will receive block grants under ESEA totaling 1.5 million dollars for the entire district, which is approximately 80 percent of the ESEA district receipts for the past fiscal year.
>
> Therefore, we have had to reevaluate programs within the district and eliminate funding for some. After extensive meetings with the Advisory Board of Funding, the Board of Education and the superintendent, we have decided to retain only the following programs at Jefferson High School: • Bilingual/Bicultural Program, • Special Education Program for the Orthopedically Impaired, • Language Arts Program for Disadvantaged Youth, and • Sex Equity Program in Vocational Education
>
> Programs that will <u>not</u> be retained under ESEA funding for the coming academic year are listed as follows: • Substance Abuse Prevention Program, and • Mathematics Laboratory Program for Disadvantaged Youth

Ted didn't even frown. Pauline had called him late last week to tell him the substance of the memo. The business office and superintendent had to submit an immediate report to the State Education Department listing specific cuts throughout the district. Pauline assured Ted that options such as the transfer of funds, other sources of funding and the use of budget surplus (if it existed) would be studied.

KEY ISSUES

A. How can the principal assure greater involvement of his staff and self in important fiscal decisions like these that affect instructional programs?

B. What options and resources are available to retain and strengthen high priority programs that are threatened by fiscal cutbacks?

SUPERVISING ASSISTANT PRINCIPALS

C. Can the principal delegate authority and responsibility to appropriate staff members—and how?
D. What procedures, criteria and follow-up actions should be planned to maximize chances for success?

ANALYSIS AND SOLUTIONS

Ted recognized that securing funding to initiate or maintain programs, projects or research had become a major activity at Jefferson High. The flow of funds from the government had reached the half-million dollar level during the previous year, but now his school (like most in the nation) would have to get by on four/fifths that amount.

He sent for Helene Hartman, his new (second year) assistant principal. She had done an outstanding job with all of her responsibilities last year and had requested more opportunities to become involved with program, budget and curriculum decisions this year. Ted reasoned correctly that Helene would be highly motivated to assume the important task of maintaining valuable and effective programs. Her professional growth had been impressive last year, and she had exhibited uncommon poise and competence as well.

Helene was delighted with the assignment and discussed strategies and procedures with Ted. She was to schedule meetings and report progress in one month.

MEMORANDUM

TO: Theodore Smith, Principal
FROM: Helene Hartman, Assistant Principal
DATE: September 15
SUBJECT: Options to Retain Funding Programs

1. <u>Elimination of Both the Substance Abuse Prevention Program and the Mathematics Laboratory Program Which Have Been in Operation for Five Years.</u>

The evaluation reports on the Substance Abuse Program for the current school year indicated that among the 250 student participants who were identified as users or potential users of dangerous substances, there was a significant improvement in attendance, attitude and behavior as observed and reported by their teachers and counselors at the conclusion of the program. The weekly counseling session apparently had proved to be effective.

Similarly, the evaluation report on the Mathematics Laboratory Program was equally positive. For the 76 student participants in Grade 10, the use of historical regression analysis and a correlated t-test showed highly significant differences between the predicted and actual posttest group scores as measured by the Metropolitan Achievement Test. (Pretest mean 5.891; predicted posttest mean 6.326; actual posttest mean 7.634; t-value 8.88; significance $p \leq .001$).

As a result, it is likely that elimination of those two programs will result in a return to previous unsatisfactory program conditions. That option is not acceptable to the staff and the Committee and is not recommended.

2. <u>Exploration of Ways to Retain the Programs by Reallocating Faculty and Resources.</u>

The major funding received for the two projects involved salaries and fringe benefits for a guidance counselor and certified secondary education mathematics teacher. It was suggested that the program activities could be reassigned to the twelve regular mathematics teachers and the seven school guidance counselors. However, meetings with those groups and the building union representatives revealed that additional classes and programs would violate the existing union contract. Moreover, even if permitted under the bargaining agreement, the proposed reallocation of assignments would not provide the concentration and continuity of the previous year and, therefore, that direction is not recommended.

3. <u>Identify Resources in the Community that Could Respond to Some of the Objectives of the Substance Abuse Prevention Program.</u>

The Director of Counseling indicated that he would assume responsibility for working with the counselors in the local community Substance Abuse Prevention and Treatment Program to develop a liaison with the school to initiate a continuing program on drug and substance education and to refer known adolescent substance abusers to the treatment programs in the community. The Committee believed that action to be feasible and potentially successful, and, therefore, unanimously recommended it.

4. <u>Explore Other Funding Sources with the District Coordinator of Funding, Faculty and Parent Representatives.</u>

This option seemed essential to the Study Committee, and with your approval I established a Math Laboratory Funding Committee consisting of two senior faculty members from the Mathematics Department, two parents employed by a major business and college in the community, and me, to work with the District Coordinator to explore potential funding sources and to develop a proposal for the remedial program in mathematics. In this regard, we have completed the following steps:

A. <u>Development of Ideas Through Brainstorming</u>

In the brainstorming session, the group members contributed thoughts on how to respond to the low achievement record of disadvantaged, adolescent students in mathematics. The following ideas were generated by group members:
- Continue the Mathematics laboratory for small groups of students and use a variety of strategies that respond to their individual learning styles based upon knowledge of their perceptual strengths, motivation, and so on.
- Incorporate the Mathematics Laboratory approach into the existing mathematics curriculum; provide in-service workshops for faculty members and include the development of creative approaches and tactual/kinesthetic materials for teaching mathematics concepts and skills.
- Lend mathematics materials and workbooks to parents and involve them more directly in helping certain youngsters.

B. <u>Project Conceptualization</u>

This step involved documenting a need for the project, defining its scope and specifying probable outcomes. When responding to the "need for the project," the Committee cited statistics related to the low achievement (both teacher grades and standardized test scores) of disadvantged students in grades 10 through 12 in mathematics. It was established, through documentation, that the needs of that special group were not being met currently through the traditional approaches to teaching mathematics.

The literature was reviewed, and studies were cited that indicated that faculty in-service workshops resulted in more innovative experimental approaches to the teaching of mathematics which, in turn, produced increased pupil achievement.

The scope of the project was defined, including the objectives for each of the workshop sessions, the use of consultants and the measurable outcomes expected for each teacher participant. A research design was selected that would compare the achievement of disadvantaged students whose teachers participated in the project with those whose teachers did not. The assessment was planned to coincide with the conclusion of the training program.

C. Proposal Writing

The Committee wrote a proposal utilizing the following outline:

I. Introduction: This section of the proposal established the credibility of the school as an organization that should be supported. Included were descriptions of significant accomplishments and organizational goals.

II. Problem Statement or Assessment of Need: This section addressed the specific problem to be solved through implementation of the program.

III. Program Objectives:: This section included anticipated, specific, measurable outcomes of the program.

IV. Methods: The process and content of the workshop sessions were clearly outlined, including the objectives and activities of each session. The resumés of experts and consultants to be employed in the training program were attached.

V. Evaluation: The evaluation design for the program was two-pronged; it measured changes in both the teacher participants and their disadvantaged students. Instruments were identified that accurately assessed the project objectives.

In this case, teachers were to be tested before and after the workshop intervention to determine whether a significant increase in knowledge was evidenced in such areas as diagnosis of student learning problems, familiarity with a broad range of strategies for teaching basic mathematical concepts and skills, and development of individualized plans remediating student deficiencies.

Second, the students of teachers who participated in the project would be compared with students whose teachers were nonparticipants; standardized achievement tests would be administered during the semester following the workshops.

VI. <u>Future Funding</u>: Increasingly, funding sources want to know whether the program will continue to exist after the grant expires. A written commitment was secured from members of the Board of Education, stating that they would fund the program through local tax monies if the outcome were quantitatively positive.

VII. <u>Budget</u>: The budget for this program included stipends for project participants, honorariums for consultants, the salary of a laboratory aide and monies for the purchase of mathematics laboratory equipment and consumable supplies including testing materials.

5. <u>Identifying Funding Sources</u>

After perusing the <u>Foundation Directory</u>, the following foundations were identified as interested in supporting educational projects:

- <u>Kellogg Foundation</u>: Particularly interested in action-oriented research that might make a difference in educational practices.
- <u>Carnegie Foundation</u>: Supports educational research projects.
- <u>Ford Foundation</u>: Particularly responsive to innovative projects and problems of inequality in education.
- <u>Rockefeller Foundation</u>: Supports educational projects at the elementary and secondary school levels.
- <u>Kettering Foundation</u>: Supports projects in the area of educational practice and leadership training.
- <u>National Science Foundation</u>: Interested in the improvement of curriculum, particularly in mathematics and science.

In addition, the Math Lab Funding Committee will explore the possibility of obtaining temporary support from local business and service organizations.

Respectfully submitted,

Helene Hartman

Helene Hartman,
Assistant Principal

HH:ibc

5
Improving Student School Participation

SITUATION 21

PROBLEM: Reacting to Student Protest

SITUATION: Case Study

by
John Swanchak and James R. Campbell

Stephen Dash became student chairperson of the Longview High School Student Council in the fall. Following a series of meetings, he, the other members of the Council, and the faculty advisor, Ms. Morris, agreed to exercise the Council's statutory right to supervise and regulate the school's after-school organizations. A memorandum was sent asking its twelve clubs and organizations to furnish a financial statement and to accept, in writing, the Student Council's authority—including the right to approve or reject fund-raising activities.

Previous Student Councils had sent out similar requests, but they had always been ignored. Traditionally, the after-school organizations had operated autonomously, and, when challenged, they had refused to respond and were allowed to maintain their independence. This time, however, despite protests, recriminations, threats of rejection and recitations of past practices, the Student Council persisted and refused to abandon its claim to authority.

Slowly and reluctantly the after-school organizations complied. Only the Longview Sentinel, the school's paper, did not. The Sentinel considered the demand an infringement on its constitutionally guaranteed freedom—in theory, if not in practice. Neither the paper's editor, John Cawz, nor its faculty advisor, Bronson Collins, would sign the statement because, they argued, it raised a First Amendment—not a student government—issue. The Student

Council's action, they insisted, was an implicit threat to the Longview Sentinel's existence as a forum for the expression of student views. Furthermore, the editor and faculty advisor noted, the paper was paid for by advertising revenue and received no funds from the Student Council.

Council members were adamant and would not yield. Stephen Dash, Student Council chairperson, and Ms. Morris, the Student Council faculty advisor, presented the Council's case to Mr. Hansen, the assistant principal. The Council's concern, Dash reported, was to unite the student body which the Council represented. Neither he nor the Council was concerned with influencing or censoring the Longview Sentinel. "They can print whatever they want," Dash said. "The important thing is that the clubs become better coordinated." Ms. Morris concurred and added that organizational efficiency and the acceptance of majority rule required that an elected Student Council, which represented all of the students, should be able to exert and have its rights upheld. "After all," she concluded, "it's not as if the Council were requiring something which is illegal or unconstitutional. This is, after all, a democracy; or is it?"

The Longview Sentinel editor and faculty advisor also met with the assistant principal, Mr. Hansen. John Cawz, the editor, contended that the paper, unlike other after-school organizations, should remain autonomous because of its role as "The Watch-Dog of the School." Any threat to the paper's independence, whether implicit or explicit, endangered the Sentinel's ability to report the activities of the school objectively and impartially and to take what might be considered unpopular positions on important school issues. "By pressuring us indirectly, they are, in fact, suppressing us," Cawz pointed out. "The student government has been impotent, and Dash is trying to restore its power, but he's doing it in a misguided way." He ended his presentation to the assistant principal by again noting that the paper received no school funds and was supported by its dedicated staff and advertising. Why, then, Cawz wanted to know, should the Longview Sentinel be required to submit to the political machinations of the Student Council?

Mr. Collins, the paper's faculty advisor, was supportive. The Student Council's proposal, he told the assistant principal, could lead to censorship. What might happen, he wondered aloud, if the Sentinel published critical or negative articles about the activities of the Student Council and then sought its approval for a fundraising activity. "It's human and understandable," Mr. Collins went on, "that we punish those who are critical or who disagree with us. The power to penalize can become an instrument for domination and control. It's as simple as that."

Mr. Collins had contacted other school paper faculty advisors in the area and the State School Press Association. All indicated surprise because a dispute between a Student Council and a school newspaper was unusual. They agreed, however, that the potential for censorship existed and that the controversy could produce a question of freedom of the press.

Following those meetings and discussions with other members of the Student Council and the Longview Sentinel, it was obvious to the assistant principal that, over a period of time, the positions of both groups had hardened. Each was certain of the correctness of its position and was enveloped in righteousness; both refused to reason or compromise. His suggestion that both groups meet with him to continue the dialogue was rejected. Instead, he was told by the Student Council chairman and the editor of the Sentinel that they expected both administrative support for their respective positions and directions to resolve the dispute. Gloomily, Mr. Hansen recognized an impasse and saw that his efforts to reach a solution provided by those involved had failed. Something had to be done, and, reluctantly, he knew that he would have to refer the dilemma to the principal.

KEY ISSUES

A. The major issue is whether the Student Council should exercise legitimate authority or permit the traditional autonomy of the school paper.

B. But, as usual, what seems simple involves a complexity of confusingly interrelated issues. These include, but are not limited to, the following questions:

1. Is there a legitimate issue of Freedom of the Press and First Amendment guarantees? Or are these claims merely efforts to maintain an independence developed because of either the ineptness or disinterest of past Student Councils? Furthermore, since time had sanctified it, was a natural reluctance to submit to inspection and review being transformed into a lofty principle?

2. Should the administration support an activist Student Council elected by the student body and hope to revive student interest in the organization which had been moribund, but which had the potential to become an agency for increasing student participation in school affairs?
3. Is there danger that an energetic Student Council might translate its mission to coordinate and either approve or disapprove of fund-raising activities into ultimate concern about articles and editorials which appeared in the Longview Sentinel?
4. What would be the impact of administrative support for one group over the other on the: (a) Student Council; (b) staff; (c) faculty advisor; and (d) quality of the paper?
5. Should the administration remain neutral, which in effect would cause the continuation of negative relationships as they currently exist?

ANALYSIS

Mr. Hansen, the assistant principal, met with the principal and they discussed the problem. They recapitulated what had happened, went over the issues and their implications, reviewed the roles and the remembered statements of the participants and examined the various decisions that could be made. "Well, what it's come to," the principal said, "is that I will have to intervene." The authority of the Student Council, he concluded, to supervise and coordinate the activities of after-school organizations, including the right to approve or reject fund-raising activities, had to be upheld.

This right was sanctioned by School Board policy, and, historically, the Student Council had regulated such student activities as the sale of soda and food at basketball and football games, car washes to raise funds for various purposes and, in the past, magazine sales to finance senior activities. Since it was elected by the student body, the Student Council, the principal argued, was the only school organization that had, at least in theory, a schoolwide constituency. Conversely, the after-school organizations consisted of students who volunteered for membership and were accepted or rejected by processes particular to each of the groups. Therefore, the essential loyalty of those members was to their group and its interests.

The Student Council, then, was the only organization that had the potential for uniting the student body and possessed the capacity for dealing with school and student issues from a broad, rather than a narrow, perspective; it also provided the necessary supervision and coordination needed for an orderly functioning of existing—or the creation of new—after-school clubs. "I'm upholding the Student Council position," the principal said, "because it is correct. Besides, any high school worth its salt should have a student government that's active." He was not concerned about the issue of Freedom of the Press. Constitutional and legal safeguards existed, the principal felt, to prevent censorship and to protect the paper as a forum for the expression of student views. Like it or not, he was aware that school officials could not prevent the publication of an article because it criticized school policies, officials or faculty or was too controversial.

The principal dismissed the threat that an overzealous Student Council might react to editorial criticism or disagreement with its policies by either curtailing or rejecting fund-raising activities requested by the paper. There were institutionl appeals and legal remedies for such situations. Moreover, since the Sentinel received no funds from the Student Council and was supported by advertising revenue, an unwanted intrusion by the Student Council into the policies and decisions of the paper was remote.

Therefore, the principal ordered the editor and the faculty advisor of the Longview Sentinel to submit a financial statement to the Student Council and to accept, in writing, the Student Council's authority—including the right to approve or reject fund-raising activities.

Until and unless that was done, the principal forbade the publication of advertisements in the paper. Compliance with the administrative order would result in the withdrawal of that prohibition.

GUIDELINES

1. Reasonable and rational authority must be communicated to all concerned and enforced based on existing policies and regulations.
2. Hearings, input and feedback should be solicited and weighed.

3. Deviations, slippage, past practice based on noncompliance, issues based on emotion, individual motives or group self-interest should be analyzed, and their impact on a final decision reduced when measured against central issues and appropriately derived authority.
4. Leadership involves responsibility for final decisions and their implementation, particularly in situations that include disputes and competing considerations.

SITUATION 22

PROBLEM: Bypassing the Chain of Command

SITUATION: Teacher's Room Observations

by
John Swanchak and James R. Campbell

It was called Junior High West and, following a period of organizational definition and redefinition, it housed grades seven, eight and nine. As in many schools, its pubescent students were garrulous, boisterous and kinetic. Also, in a sports-conscious community, most of the students were obsessed with dreams of becoming members of school-sponsored teams. Ninth grade boys who were chosen for junior varsity teams and ninth grade girls who became junior varsity cheerleaders acquired instant prestige and an envied status.

For years, Miss Mary Byrnes had been the faculty director of the school's cheer leaders. She was a native of the community, educated in its schools, and, after being graduated from the State

University, had returned to become a secondary school physical education teacher. Miss Byrnes gave generously of her time to school affairs, to students and to her church. She was admired and respected by the school's administration and faculty and by friends and acquaintances in the community.

Following the series of spring tryouts for junior varsity cheerleaders, word quickly spread that Penny Graham, a ninth grader, had not been selected. Penny's friends were outraged, but, among certain youngsters, the news was a source of malicious glee and unobtrusive derision. Like the students, the faculty was both amazed and amused. Generally, those who had taught Penny Graham felt she was socially mature and aware beyond her years— an average student whose expectations exceeded her ability and effort. On occasion, some of them had perceived her as arrogant and demanding. This "incident," they agreed, would be a severe test of the skills and the mettle of Mr. Shaw, the principal. "I'm glad it's him," a faculty member commented, "and not me." "He'd better be a silver-tongued orator," another said, "or he's in deep, deep trouble." The situation became the main topic of conversation in the faculty room.

Mr. Shaw had begun his second year as principal of Junior High West. He had been selected from outside the system by a district search committee that had bypassed two West faculty candidates whose friends whispered that the best had been overlooked. Mr. Shaw's personal agenda upon becoming principal was to review administrative practices and the curricular structure, to assess the faculty, and to get, as he termed it, "a feel of the school." He had been away during the trials for junior varsity cheerleaders, and upon his return, the assistant principal, a younger member of the faculty whom he had appointed, told him of the rumblings among students and faculty about the junior varsity cheerleader selection. The assistant principal, however, was not alarmed and felt that, although there would be some "noise," the incident would soon be forgotten.

During that conversation, his secretary interrupted and informed Mr. Shaw that the superintendent wanted to meet with him in the early afternoon if it was convenient.

The superintendent was a tall, massively built man with thinning grey hair. He had headed the district for nine years. He enjoyed being superintendent and had privately and publicly said that he wanted to continue until he retired. After the usual pleasantries, he told Mr. Shaw that he had been called by Mr. Graham,

Penny's father, and by Mr. Loomis, the Board president; he had been questioned about the selection process for junior varsity cheerleaders. "Frank Graham and Will Loomis," the superintendent said, "are friends and devoted supporters of the school." He asked Mr. Shaw to "check things out" and report to him. "Sometimes," the superintendent concluded, "little things can get out of hand. Let's get control of this situation."

When he returned to the Junior High School, Mr. Shaw met with Miss Byrnes. She was aware that Penny Graham was upset because Mrs. Graham had called her. Miss Byrnes told the principal what she had told Mrs. Graham. The criteria for selection were published and well known. The judgments were made by a committee consisting of Mr. Brand, Miss Kinsten, both physical education teachers, and herself. Although she previously had spoken to Penny and her friends about the time it took them to change for gym classes and their reluctance to participate in physical education activities—other than dance—Miss Byrnes assured the principal, as she had Mrs. Graham, that those encounters had not been factors in the decision. "What really irritates me," she said, "was Mrs. Graham's wondering about the selection of 'plain' Beth Johnson. What she really meant was that Beth lives on the wrong side of the tracks. Well, for her information, Beth is a bright kid, a good kid and a fine athlete. That's why she was chosen!"

That afternoon, Mr. Shaw received a phone call from Mrs. Graham asking him if he would come to the Graham home that evening for a drink and a chat. He agreed and arrived at seven. Mr. Graham was a prominent attorney and involved in local politics. After initial greetings and brief inconsequential social conversation, the principal was offered—and accepted—a drink.

Mr. Graham began to discuss the issue by saying he was concerned about Penny. "I've known Mary Byrnes all of my life," he noted. "She's a fine person and gives of herself, but she can be rigid and puritanical. She's come a long way from her beginnings, but still, there are certain people she resents." Mrs. Graham hoped that Mr. Shaw did not think they were interfering. Rather, her husband and she had always encouraged their children to perform well academically and to participate in school activities. Penny's older brother and sister had been school leaders and had done very well in life. Penny, too, would be an asset to the community someday. An uncomfortable Mr. Shaw thanked them for their interest and, after a decent interval, left.

The next day Mr. Shaw asked Penny to come to his office. She was tall for her age, slender and attractive. Penny greeted the principal politely, but unlike many of her age group, her poise indicated that she was neither awed nor threatened by an adult in authority. She told the principal that she respected and admired Miss Byrnes and that, although disappointed, she accepted the judgment made about her inability to be a cheerleader. "There will be another time," she said with a smile, "and maybe I'll be selected."

Next, the principal met with Mr. Brand and Miss Kinsten, the other members of the committee involved in the selection. They vehemently defended Miss Byrnes and the choice that had been made. The criteria were clear, fair and objective, they insisted, and they gave the principal a copy of the evaluation form and asked him to review it. Finally, the principal went to the office of Mr. Hodiak, the director of Health and Physical Education. He was an older man who had spent his entire professional career in the school system. The director and the superintendent had been college classmates and were life-long friends. The principal asked Mr. Hodiak about his views of the problem. "I am proud of the professional competence of our staff," the director replied, "and I never question decisions they make so long as procedures are followed. That's why morale is so high and why we don't get the back-biting among my people that they do in other departments. I've lived by that principle, and it works." Mr. Shaw thanked the director for his remarks and returned to his office.

KEY ISSUES

   A. *If the decision were reversed*:
   1. Would organizational procedures have to be modified? Would such action insure the selection of Penny Graham?
   2. Would it permanently alienate most of the faculty or would they eventually forget it as other incidents and issues developed?
   3. Given the controversy that would erupt, how supportive would the superintendent be?
   B. *If the decision were upheld*:
   1. Would this affect the tenure decision on Mr. Shaw that had to be made by the superintendent and the Board of Education?

2. Would it permanently rupture an amicable relationship with the superintendent and compromise Mr. Shaw's ability to lead the school effectively?
3. What help would the faculty provide, and would there be elements of the community that would support it?

C. *If the decision were reviewed*:
1. Might it not be argued that a judgment about the fairness and equity of the decision should be made by the director of Health and Physical Education and that he be administratively ordered to do so?
2. Could it be argued that such a delicate and sensitive issue required an objective and dispassionate review and that the appropriate instrument for the task was an administrative-faculty committee?

ANALYSIS

During the weekend, Mr. Shaw reviewed the possible options he had and weighed the pros and cons of each. In the sorting, he rejected the administrative alternative of requesting that the director of Health and Physical Education decide whether the decision should be upheld or rejected; he was aware that Mr. Hodiak either could appeal to the superintendent to countermand it or, possibly, refuse to comply and insist that he was being asked to do something he had no authority to do. Such an impasse would have to be resolved by the superintendent who probably would support the director.

The principal also dismissed the creation of an administrative-faculty committee to review the decision. He thought that such a step might be regarded as an attempt to place the burden of judging upon others; that might be construed as his being fearful or weak (or both); it might also be regarded by the superintendent as a device to subvert his wish for a speedy and an appropriate resolution of the incident.

He spent hours that weekend wrestling with the motives of others—a process that invariably leads to uncertain conclusions. Was it possible that a hidden motive, perhaps not even recognized, was the basis of the decision-making that concerned Penny Graham? The principal knew that Miss Byrnes' father had labored until he retired for a local concern owned by the Graham family.

Like so many others, Mary Byrnes had worked and striven to rise above her previous economic station and had succeeded; some who had struggled might resent those who had experienced smoother and easier roads to success. The Grahams believed that, given the opportunity to choose and the ambiguity of criteria, Miss Byrnes had selected a student who was like her and had rejected a student who was not. While that might be plausible, the principal concluded, it could not be verified. Although motives might be questioned, that certainly was an insufficient basis for objective administrative decision-making.

The principal wondered, too, about pupil-teacher relationships and the incident. Apparently, Miss Byrnes was not very fond of Penny Graham, but other members of the faculty also were not fond of her. Teacher discussions about the behaviors, characteristics and abilities of students occur in every school, are invevitable and are probably necessary if used constructively. But attempts to trace its influence and predict its results are difficult and tenuous. In a particular context, then, there is simply no way of knowing whether a teacher's decision is determined by a student's reputation among the faculty or whether it emerges solely from the conditions of the situation. Therefore, the principal dismissed "the reputation concept" as a factor in determining what he should do.

After hours of questioning and arranging issues and options, the principal decided that he had to support the Committee's decision in the selection of cheerleaders. On Monday he would meet with the superintendent and explain why he had decided as he did and tell him what he intended to do. Since his examination had exposed neither procedural violations nor demonstrable evidence of bias, he would not intervene. Additionally, an item-by-item analysis of the evaluation instrument used by the Committee revealed that it appeared to have been fair and objective. He also would tell the superintendent that he would communicate his decision in writing to Mary Byrnes, the director of Health and Physical Education and the Grahams. Finally, he would see Penny Graham and tell her. He would encourage her, too, to continue her efforts to participate in cheerleading or any other school activity.

GUIDELINES

1. Criteria for selection to teams or any school-sponsored function should be written as objectively as possible, com-

municated clearly and accurately to students and made available to faculty and parents.
2. Judgments for selection should be consistent with the criteria and should involve a small jury or a faculty sponsor plus two or more advisors whenever appropriate.
3. Perceptions of motives, assessments of bias, transfers of performance from another context, attitudes, personality conflicts and pressures or influences should not be allowed to modify objective decisions.
4. Periodic review of procedures tends to improve objective assessments.

SITUATION 23

PROBLEM: Dealing with the Rebel Without a Cause

SITUATION: Letters from Students

by
John Swanchak and James R. Campbell

After dealing with the major and minor problems associated with the daily opening of school and the beginning of classes, Mr. Wetsel, the principal of Brookville High School, invariably retreated to the privacy of his office to examine his unread mail. The first letter he chose was addressed to "The Principal" and did not include the usual "Mr. Stanley Wetsel." That puzzled him and piqued his curiosity about the contents. He opened the letter.

> Dear Herr Fuhrer, Master of the Fourth Reich:
>
> Since, through the usual establishment tactics of intrigue, scheming, croneyism and lackeyism, you became the head administrator of this school, the Coordinating Committee for Democracy and Social Justice has watched you impose a Fascist regime upon the student body. We know that you are a puppet of a power structure which is corrupt, decadent and anti-progressive. This is to warn you to BEWARE! This student body will not be suppressed or repressed in the struggle for freedom and individuality. Students will stand up for their rights regardless of the consequences. OUR DEMANDS WILL FOLLOW!
>
> The Committee

The words aroused memories of another time and place, of Vietnam and student unrest and the fumblings of a beginning teacher. They amused rather than annoyed him. Mr. Wetsel had been an assistant principal who then succeeded the principal who had retired. He had been chosen to impose order upon a school which, a community consensus insisted, suffered from excessive problems of absenteeism, class-cutting, vandalism, student violence and drugs. Upon becoming principal, Mr. Wetsel closed the student lounge, increased hall and lavatory monitoring, tightened the student accounting system to assure class attendance and developed a student handbook in which procedures for school infractions were carefully detailed. The most controversial of those was that if a student was suspected of possessing drugs, he or she would be searched. If drugs were found, parents and the police would be notified. Generally, those actions were supported by the Board of Education and the superintendent, the Parent-Teacher Association, most of the faculty and many of the students.

The principal phoned the superintendent about the letter and informally discussed it with various members of the staff and faculty. When asked about what he intended to do, his reply was that he would wait. Several days later a second letter arrived.

> Dear Herr Fuhrer:
>
> Because we are representative of the total student body, our demands must be met without exception. If they are not, the

> responsibility for the terrible consequences which will follow are yours alone.
>
> In the name of the students and their right to freedom and individuality: (1) Student rights to assemble and to exercise free speech must be respected; (2) Suspension and expulsion must be eliminated; (3) No dress code should be imposed; (4) Relevant courses should be introduced; (5) A student's right to privacy cannot be violated, and (6) <u>The Student Lounge Must be Reopened</u>!
>
> We expect your announcement of your unconditional acceptance of these demands in the next issue of <u>The Lamplighter.</u>
>
> The Coordinating Committee
for Democracy and Social Justice

The principal weighed these words and their implications. He wondered about the tactics that might be used to escalate attention to their cause and demands. Would it be destructive acts of vandalism such as firecrackers, the use of spray paint, or arson? It was not inconceivable that they might strike at his personal property or family. Such, he mourned, augured a time when innocence was no more, when one merely accepted that the young were capable of violence and villainy. On the other hand, was this merely a diabolic prank?—a joke that would amuse and enthrall the pranksters and their friends and then quietly pass because other diversions would catch their interest? He begrudged them their joy but wished it were true, since it would simply and harmlessly resolve unpleasantness and danger.

Try as he would, Mr. Wetsel could not persuade himself that this convenient explanation was so. He concluded that the words were too strident, too impassioned and too reasoned to be only a prank. The language cleverly appealed to the puritanical righteousness and moral absolutism of adolescents and tied them to issues that would attract some groups of students.

The principal decided to call Lt. Gomberti, a police department friend, to seek his impressions. He outlined what had occurred and what he had surmised. The Lieutenant listened, had nothing to add and agreed that the letters could lead to serious trouble. He was sympathetic and said that the high school "... had more than its fair share of loonies and crazies."

The Lieutenant wondered, too, if the principal suspected anyone. Mr. Wetsel remembered his meetings with Joyce Karamon, a senior who had been sent to him for using abusive and vulgar language, defying and taunting several of her teachers and smoking in stairwells and lavatories. She was barely five feet tall, was clothed in apparel from the army surplus store, and was suspicious, articulate and unrepentant. During her three previous years at the school, Joyce had never been a problem and was academically outstanding. Then, teachers had reported that late in her junior year she had become deeply committed to "liberal causes," had demonstrated for a variety of them and had been arrested with others for attempting to seize and shut down a local nuclear generating plant. Joyce had become, those teachers said, "a different person." In fact, she was a member of a group that one English teacher had labeled, "The Bloomsberry Set"—intellectual youngsters from affluent homes who were reputed to be "swingers and into dope." It was also reported that they tolerated and encouraged exotic and unusual behavior.

Although Joyce had been identified with the "Bloomies," she had many friends and was accepted within other student groups. In her sessions with the principal, she defended her behavior with vehemence and skill. When the principal had told her that her arrogance and rudeness could be neither tolerated nor condoned and that if she persisted and refused to change, she would jeopardize being graduated with her class, her reply was: "You have to do what you have to do, and I have to do what I have to do." He recognized the iron in her and sensed a romantic's or ideologue's quest and yearning for recognition. This young lady, he knew, could be a formidable adversary. The principal said nothing about his discussions with Joyce to Lt. Gomberti. The Lieutenant ended their conversation by advising him to stay calm and promising that police patrols of the high school and its environs would be intensified.

Later that morning, a younger member of the faculty came to his office and showed him copies of letters which he said were circulating among the students. This teacher had received them from a student who had asked for confidentiality. When the principal asked about the potential influence of the letters, the teacher said that the student who had read them did not want to become involved but was waiting to see what would happen.

While walking to the faculty cafeteria, Mr. Wetsel was stopped by an older teacher who asked if he was aware that the students were talking about certain letters and whispering about their "lost freedoms" and doing something about it. She told him that she resented those teachers who joked about "applying for combat pay," that she and other teachers were fearful of violence and that she was furious with those of the younger faculty who empathized with the students. She felt that lack of professionalism should be reprimanded. The monologue was interrupted by his secretary who informed him that the superintendent had called and wanted to be contacted immediately.

KEY ISSUES

A. Should the letters from the Coordinating Committee for Democracy and Social Justice be ignored, and, except for an expansion and intensification of the faculty monitoring system, nothing be done? What would be the reaction of the Coordinating Committee, the faculty, and the student body to a strategy of waiting for an overt act before responding?

B. Given the growing agitation among the students and the rising apprehensions of faculty, should the superintendent be advised that a threat to the safety and security of students and faculty exists and that police presence should be requested?

C. Should a faculty meeting be called to discuss the problem and an attempt be made to develop a consensual administrative-faculty policy that would be recommended to the superintendent for implementation?

D. Should the student body be convened in an assembly, the events and their consequences outlined, and an appeal made to the students for support against those who threatened to disrupt the school? Should the students be warned that involvement in a movement to create anarchy would be penalized and noted on their records and that it would affect employment referrals, athletic and scholastic awards and college recommendations?

E. Should he meet with Joyce Karamon, reveal his suspicions about her, accuse her of being the inventor of the obsessions of the Coordinating Committee, charge her with being the major author of the letters, and advise her that she and her friends would be suspended for any infraction of school rules?

F. Should he reply to the letters in *The Lamplighter* as he had been asked and wait for the next occurrence? What would be the reaction of the Coordinating Committee, the faculty and the students to this response from him?

ANALYSIS

Mr. Wetsel returned to his office and considered the above alternative actions. He knew that at this point something had to be done. Doing nothing might be interpreted by the Coordinating Committee as a lack of backbone and might imply that the initiative for determining what would occur was theirs. That might incite the Committee members to increase their pressure through acts that would be meant to serve as symbols of the powerlessness of the principal and their contempt for him. Increasing tensions could possibly lead to emulation by uninvolved but unstable students. Moreover, if nothing was done, the faculty, whose support he needed, would be adrift, and rumors, half-truths and their imaginations would intensify fears and apprehensions. That would only aggravate their concerns that things might get out of control.

The principal dismissed the possibility of involving the police. The presence of uniformed officers would be a concession that he and the faculty could not provide the necessary order and security and would damage the custom of student acceptance of authority from school personnel. Without positive school climate, good education would not be possible. Although some of the faculty would applaud police patrols, others would resent them. They would rightfully regard such action as a diminution of their professional competence and an intrusion by an outside agency. The presence of police also would confirm what the Coordinating Committee had threatened—that the "illegitimate suppression" of student rights and freedoms could be sustained only by force. And, finally, police patrols would frighten parents and confirm the impressions of the lunatic fringe in the community who would insist that the high school was a den of wickedness and depravity.

The principal decided, too, against calling a faculty meeting to discuss the problem. There was too large a faculty in the school to examine the entangling issues rationally. What would probably happen at such a meeting was that vocal extremists among the faculty would dominate; from one faction there would be a demand to get tough, to suspend the malcontents and to end "permissiveness." From another faction would come pleas for compassion and understanding and hints about the consequences of authoritarianism and its impact upon the development of authentic personalities. Such an exchange would merely alarm or enrage the uncommitted among the faculty and end any appearance of administrative-faculty unity.

The convening of a student assembly also would not serve any useful purpose. The principal was aware that many of the twelve hundred students knew nothing about what was happening. Thus, a plea for student support by him would be unintelligible to some, confusing to others and would be greeted by derisive giggles and malicious epigrams from those who resented authority. Those unintended effects of his address, then, could do more harm than good.

He would not, he decided, as several of the faculty had suggested, "read the riot act to the kids." Threats would merely heighten fears and anxieties or arouse latent hostilities and induce sullenness and reprisals.

Mr. Wetsel considered confronting Joyce Karamon, but he was certain that she would either deny his inferences and allegations or would smile ambiguously and tell him to provide proof and to press charges or leave her alone. In such a situation the advantage would be hers. She would be neither intimidated nor frightened; she knew there was little he could do without evidence. In that moment of contemplation, the principal admitted to himself his admiration of the mistaken, misguided, but resourceful, young opponent.

To prepare for his meeting with the superintendent, Mr. Wetsel decided to outline what he would say. He would explain why he did not want police presence, why he rejected either meeting with the faculty or convening the student body and why he could not confront those he suspected. Instead, he proposed to reply to the letters in *The Lamplighter*. In his response he would defend his administrative actions, would rebut the contentions of the Coordinating Committee and would reaffirm that current school policy would continue. Students would be suspended, and, if the facts warranted it, recommended for expulsion for violations of school rules. Each of the faculty would be informed, in writing, of what he planned to do.

In addition, he would encourage a more active Student Council to assure representation from all student groups. He would outline plans to meet with the Student Council, department chairpersons, status teachers, guidance personnel and assistant principals to discuss cooperative decisions concerning discipline and vandalism, conditions for reopening the student lounge, student involvement in community ventures and other positive student/faculty actions.

GUIDELINES

1. Involve respected and wise faculty members, administrators, police officers, students and others as a sounding board during difficult situations or periods.
2. Consider all options, weigh the potential consequences of each path, and select the one that is most positive, constructive and in keeping with the goals of the school and the well-being of students and faculty.
3. Retain authority and control, but exercise leadership by involving key personnel and students in continuing efforts to maintain positive and constructive cooperation by all concerned.

SITUATION 24

PROBLEM: Handling the Disputed Grade

SITUATION: Confrontation

by
William McLaughlin

Charles Judd, principal of the Fourth Street High School, was working feverishly on the budget that was due in the superintendent's office at the close of the school day. The quiet of the General

IMPROVING STUDENT SCHOOL PARTICIPATION

Office was broken by the sound of Mr. Babcock's voice demanding: "Is Dr. Judd in? I've got to see him right away!" Judd didn't wait to be summoned by his secretary. He put aside the budget forms he had been working on and headed for the General Office. When he opened the door, he saw Mr. Babcock, the head custodian, standing in a puddle of water that dripped from his drenched clothing. Beside him, and equally wet, was Jerry Hendricks, a senior at the school.

"What happened?" Judd asked.

"I was passing the boys' room on the second floor when I heard this terrific crash! I went into the lavoratory, and this here kid was ripping the washbasin off the wall. The place is a mess! There's water everywhere. I have George up there now trying to clean it up. We may have to close it for the rest of the week."

"Thank you, Mr. Babcock. I personally appreciate your diligence and concern, and I know the entire staff feels the same way. Now, why don't you get out of those wet clothes?"

Turning to Jerry Hendricks, Dr. Judd asked, "Have you gym clothes in your locker?"

"Yes, sir," Jerry replied.

"Why don't you go and change and then come back here?"

A few minutes later Jerry was back in the office in his gym shorts, sneakers and T-shirt.

"Come into my office," Dr. Judd commanded.

When they were inside the office, Dr. Judd asked Jerry to tell him what happened. His account of the incident was in substantial agreement with Mr. Babcock's report. That was surprising, for Jerry was not a troublemaker, and, indeed, was one of the better students at the school.

"Well, Jerry, I'm going to have to suspend you for a week. What's your phone number? I'll have to call your parents."

Dr. Judd spoke with Mrs. Hendricks on the phone, explained the situation, informed her that Jerry was suspended for a week, and suggested that she bring a pair of dry trousers and a plastic bag to carry his wet clothing home.

At the end of the quarter, teachers turned in the student grades for the period. Grades for all students suspended during the quarter were segregated and automatically lowered to seventy percent. School policy required that such students could receive no higher grade. For Jerry, this meant all of his grades (which were ninety percent or better) automatically were lowered to seventy percent.

KEY ISSUE

The central issue in this case is the accuracy of the messages schools transmit concerning student scholastic achievement. More basically, what does a report card report?

A common occurrence in secondary schools is the student who reports to gym class unprepared; some piece of required equipment has been left at home. In such cases may schools legitmately lower the student's grade and even deny him a high school diploma because of failure to report for class with appropriate attire?

Another extension of the difficulties associated with reporting student achievement occurs when the homogeneous grouping or tracking of students is practiced. Is it possible for a student in the lowest track of a subject area to get an A in that course while a student in the upper track of the same subject, who conceivably knows considerably more of the content in that area, receives a C simply because he is in a class with greater demands or higher standards?

Obviously, the issue is "What is a report card reporting?" Is it the absolute amount that a student has achieved of a designated amount of cognitive information or the relative amount of information according to his individual capacity?

The issue is exacerbated in the case of students with learning disabilities who have been mainstreamed and for whom individual educational programs (IEPs) have been developed. What is reported if these students achieve each of the annual goals and short-term instruction objectives outlined in the IEPs—even when their goals and objectives are substantially different from those of their classmates? Obviously, the situation is not restricted to mainstreamed students but involves all students in individualized programs. How are reports of the actual achievement of individuals transmitted and interpreted? How does one report the differences between the achievement of two fourth grade students, one of whom achieves all the objectives that are individually prescribed for him although they are at the second grade level, and another who achieves all the objectives that are individually prescribed for him when his objectives are at a sixth grade level?

How should reports of student achievement based on individual criteria—as opposed to a common standard—be evaluated by other agencies and institutions to which students may apply for employment or admission?

ANALYSIS

The Monday morning following the distribution of grades, Mr. Hendricks, Jerry's father, was waiting to see Dr. Judd. He agreed that his son's actions were wrong and that the suspension was justified, but challenged the right of the school automatically to lower a teacher's evaluation of a student's academic achievement because of misconduct. He insisted that conduct and achievement were separate, unrelated matters and should be reported and dealt with separately. Indeed, it would have been appropriate for Jerry to pay for the damage he had caused or to work for the school, he suggested, but that reduced grades were an inappropriate penalty.

Dr. Judd agreed that Mr. Hendricks' arguments had merit, but insisted that as long as the school policy required lowering grades of students suspended during the quarter to seventy percent, he had to administer this policy.

The Hendricks family retained an attorney who presented their case to the State Commissioner of Education. The Commissioner agreed with the Hendricks' position and ordered the school district to correct its records so that the report of scholastic achievement would be accurate and not reflect adjustment of a student's record of academic attainment based on factors other than scholarship.

GUIDELINES

1. Grades for individual student performance should be based on the achievement of assigned academic goals and scholastic standards that are clearly and accurately communicated to students and parents.
2. Grades should be assigned consistently and fairly, based on student performance and outcomes.
3. The assessment of scholastic achievement and the assignment of grades should not be modified by noncognitive concerns such as poor behavior, or used as a weapon to enforce discipline.

SITUATION 25

> **PROBLEM:** Helping the Student Who Fails to Pass Competency Exams
>
> **SITUATION:** Child Study Team

by
John Swanchak and James R. Campbell

Mr. Harthorne's tenth grade math classes are always intense affairs for his students; he has great reserves of energy, always assigns the most homework, gives the most difficult tests and requires the most participation. It is easy for a student to hide and become just another face in the crowd in most classes in this large urban high school, but not in Mr. Harthorne's classes. He learns all their names in the first few days and thereafter freely calls on them to explain how to solve various math problems. What's more, Mr. Harthorne becomes noticeably upset with students who don't respond well to his questions.

Jason Jackson, although not a troublemaker, doesn't seem to have many friends and "hangs out" outside the building every chance he gets. You often see him standing just beyond the exit doors between periods or at lunch time, but he never arrives at school early and never stays afterward for any event.

Things take a serious turn when Jason fails the newly required basic state competency test in math. Unless he can pass that test, he will not be graduated from high school. Mr. Harthorne outlines a program of remediation for all those who failed the test, but Jason shows no interest in attempting the extra work. He doesn't do the assignments, fails the class tests and isn't able to participate in any of the related discussions. His only observable reaction has been to

IMPROVING STUDENT SCHOOL PARTICIPATION

ask for a transfer to another math class. Jason claims that Mr. Harthorne hates him.

After considering the situation, the guidance counselor decides that there is no factual basis behind that claim; Jason's subsequent failure of the competency exam reinforces that conclusion. He sees no reason to transfer a youngster who won't work for a grade. The counselor also reports that he has been unable to reach anyone at Jason's home. Every call terminates with only a series of rings; no one ever seems to be home either during the school day or as late as 8:00 p.m.

The principal, Ms. Harriet Stone, likes to remain aloof from such problems, but the Board of Education has been making an issue of the number of students who failed the State Basic Competency Test. Board members have voiced the fear that each failure will be cited as evidence of the district's overall decline. In point of fact, the district's mean College Board scores have decreased during the last ten years by twenty points in math and forty points in verbal competency. The media recently carried several stories about national academic declines, and a number of groups in this community have become concerned and have discussed the issue at Board meetings. There is apprehension about the information concerning the competency failures being published in the two local newspapers. If that happened, Ms. Stone would certainly be called upon to explain how the problem is being handled at her high school.

After thinking about the situation, Ms. Stone decides to have a meeting with both Mr. Harthorne and Jason. She has several questions that must be answered. First, is Mr. Harthorne just generally too insensitive to youngsters who don't learn easily? Or, rather, is he merely antagonistic toward Jason as an individual? On the other hand, he is the most dynamic math teacher in the school. Could his remediation program be used to help certain youngsters pass the exam, and perhaps not others? Ms. Stone also wonders why no one is ever home at Jason's. Where are his parents? Is there a problem of which the school should be aware?

The meeting takes place during lunch period on a rainy day and doesn't resolve the problem. Ms. Stone is not able to find any evident animosity between Mr. Harthorne and Jason. In fact, Jason seems to admit that the problem is his own lack of effort. Mr. Harthorne doesn't mount any major attack, and Jason remains basically uncommunicative. When Ms. Stone asks Jason why his parents can't be reached, he says that his mother works and that his father has been away for some time. Despite several tactful questions, Ms. Stone isn't able to obtain any additional information. After the meeting, Ms. Stone looks out at the gloomy weather which seems to match her own mood. Her alternatives seem clear as she tries to examine this problem:

1. Do nothing;
2. Transfer Jason to another math teacher;
3. Assist in developing a better relationship between Jason and Mr. Harthorne; or
4. Develop a remediation program.

KEY ISSUES

A. What should the Board and the central administration do about the community's view of declining quality?
B. Was the school actually failing to identify and prescribe for underachievers?
C. Was this teacher insensitive to the needs of this student?
D. How should a school deal with apathetic students or parents?

ANALYSIS

Ms. Stone carefully considered each of the alternatives. To do nothing had several advantages; certainly it was the easiest option. After all, the student and his parents really didn't seem too concerned, and Mr. Harthorne didn't appear to actually dislike this student; it was possible that the semester might end without too much friction. Mr. Harthorne's behavior toward selected students might really be "more bark than bite." As to those who had failed the basic competency test, all the neighboring districts had about the same failure rate. Furthermore, the falling test scores on the College Board Exam were also a problem in all the surrounding districts. It really was a national problem—probably caused more by the breakdown of the family unit than by anything the schools did. The counselor's inability to contact Jason's parents was a prime example. Ms. Stone concluded that the community and the board would probably be satisfied with that explanation.

The second alternative had some positive elements. By transferring Jason, it might be possible to remove Mr. Harthorne from his pulpit. That would quiet matters at faculty meetings whenever the topic of falling scores arose. Mr. Harthorne had been using Jason as an example of what was wrong and why students were failing the Basic Compentency Exam. He kept demanding that the school should get tougher and raise its standards. Ms. Stone usually argued that such a solution was just not possible in today's world. If Jason were transferred, would Mr. Harthorne really quiet down? Ms. Stone doubted that he would. Would any benefit come to Jason by transferring him? Certainly he'd be happy to be away from all the Harthorne pressure, but the end result could be even more apathy and less work. In short, transferring Jason might do him more harm than good.

Ms. Stone then seriously considered the third alternative—working on both antagonists to modify their positions. After some analysis, she came to the conclusion that it just wouldn't work. Throughout her six years as principal, she had found Mr. Harthorne to be an inflexible man. Each attempt to move him off center seemed to force him into an even more rigid position. He seemed to believe that his mathematical ability had made him a more logical and objective human being. That feeling of superiority made it difficult for others to show him that his own position might actually be contributing to the problem.

Was it possible to mollify Jason? In truth, Jason was apathetic about everything related to school. As the psychologist has pointed out, there was nothing physically or psychologically wrong with the boy. "His mind is just elsewhere." Ms. Stone came to the conclusion that the counselor also was right about the transfer; Jason really seemed to just want to "loaf in peace."

It was for those reasons that Ms. Stone settled on developing a remediation program despite the fact that such a program would involve several serious problems. For one thing, there were no funds in the current budget for this type of program. How could she get people to work on such an effort without being paid? Furthermore, how could this type of program attack the apathy of students like Jason? Obviously, Mr. Harthorne's plan would be a beginning, but the input of many others was needed to make the program effective. At what time of day could such a program be implemented? Jason and the other students like him would certainly not volunteer to attend after school. The program must be so constituted that it could fit into the regular school day. That would require much imagination.

One obvious reason for selecting that alternative was to avoid any criticism of the school by the Board or the community. Of greater importance, the remediation program could later be enlarged to include some of the competencies included in the College Board Exams; in that way perhaps the annual decline in scores could be arrested. That would be a major accomplishment. However, the failures on the competency test and the declining scores on the College Board Exam involved mutually exclusive populations. The former represented the lowest achieving group in the school, and the latter involved the college-bound students.

Ms. Stone realizes that each problem requires a different solution, but that a remediation program might be a step in the right direction for both. In any event, she called key teachers, department chairpersons, guidance counselors, the psychologist and social workers to form Child Study Teams and to design special remediation programs for math underachievers.

GUIDELINES

List and rate the following administrative goals in order of priority:

a. Helping each student to achieve success, to feel positive about school and self and to develop independence skills;
b. Providing staff motivation, opportunities to succeed with students, and good working conditions;
c. Communicating and interacting with the community and central office on issues and perceptions;
d. Communicating with all concerned and assessing positions and attitudes objectively;
e. Involving all concerned in constructive efforts to eliminate any problem facing an individual student, teacher or any school group.

The answers are at the bottom of this page.

Answers: a, b, e, d, c.

6

Motivating the Teaching Staff

SITUATION 26

PROBLEM: Stimulating a Veteran Faculty to Reach Marginal Students

SITUATION: A Written Proposal from the Guidance Department

by
Shirley A. Griggs

TO: Mr. Robert Sage
FROM: Ava N. Site, Guidance Department Coordinator
SUBJECT: Proposal to Reach Marginal Students

Nearly twenty percent of our students during the past five years have failed to complete graduation requirements here at Grant High School. Ninety percent of that group dropped out of school last year!

At your request, we surveyed as many of the dropout youngsters as we could locate; the most serious problem appears to be a basic conflict with the conventional school environment.

We polled the teachers, too, and they described a series of stages that such students appear to pass through:

1. Loss of interest in school followed by low or failing grades.

2. Cutting of classes, unauthorized absences and eventual confrontations with administrators.

3. Disruptive and rebellious behavior, suspensions and subsequent meetings with parents and deans of discipline.

4. Increased defensiveness and negativism as parents become involved.

Let's examine a typical, potential dropout.

John D. is 16 years of age and enrolled in his sophomore year at our high school. Perusal of his cumulative record and counseling folder reveals the following data:

Background Information: John is a male Caucasian, second generation Italian-American of lower middle class background.

Family Background: John's father is 38 years of age and employed as an assembly line worker in a wheel and ball bearing manufacturing plant. He completed the equivalent of sixth grade in Italy, and his family migrated to the United States in 1955. His mother is a 36-year-old housewife who completed the eighth grade. John has four siblings: Ann, aged 15, Dominic, aged 13, Carl, aged 10, and Maria, aged 6.

Educational History: John has attended six schools due to family mobility. He was retained in the second grade. School attendance records are as follows:

School	Grades	Years Attended	Days Absent
Carlyle Elementary	1,2	1970-73	30
Lincoln Elementary	3	1973-74	10
Richard Elementary	4,5	1974-76	25
Becker Intermediate	6,7	1976-78	28
Pierce Junior High	8	1978-79	14
Washington High	9,10	1979-81	54

Health Record: John is 5½ feet in height and weighs 150 pounds. He had a variety of childhood diseases including mumps, chicken pox and measles. He has a minor loss of hearing in the left ear. His frequent absences from school were attributed primarily to dental problems and influenza.

Achievement Record:

Grades 1-6: Retained in Grade 2 for two years.
Grades in Reading and Mathematics: Poor.
Grades in Social Studies and Science: Satisfactory.

Grade 7:	Reading	D	Social Studies	C
	Mathematics	D	English	D
	General Science	C	Physical Education	B
Grade 8:	Reading	D	Social Studies	C
	Mathematics	D	English	D
	General Science	D	Physical Education	C

Grade 9:	Spanish	F	Biology	D
	English	D	General Shop	D
	General Mathematics	F	Physical Education	C

Standardized Test Scores (Secondary Level): 3/78

Grade 7: Iowa Test of Educational Development
- Reading 4.5 grade level
- Mathematics 5.0 grade level
- Science 4.6 grade level
- Social Studies 4.5 grade level
- Language Arts 4.0 grade level

Grade 8: Differential Aptitude Tests 3/79 (Percentiles)

Verbal reasoning	10	Mechanical reasoning	52
Numerical ability	22	Space relations	48
VR and NA	15	Spelling	30
Abstract reasoning	28	Language usage	25
Clerical	35		

Grade 9: Stanford Achievement Tests 3/80

Vocabulary	5.2	Spelling	5.9
Reading comprehension	4.4	Social Science	5.5
		Science	5.8
Math concepts	5.8	Listening Comprehension	4.0
Math computation	6.0		

Grade 9: Mooney Problem Check List 3/80

> A total of 45 problems were checked with the greatest number in the following areas: health and physical development, social-psychological relations, home and family, adjustment to school.

Personality Characteristics: John is extremely introverted and has difficulty relating to both peers and adults. He appears despondent most of the time and shows a lack of interest in academic areas. He lacks goals and seems to be unable to commit himself to anything. He describes his primary interests as watching television (particularly sports events), motorcycling and fishing.

Counselor Anecdotal Notes:
9/15/82

Mr. Perone, John's English teacher, referred his case, pointing out frequent cutting, failure to submit homework assignments and general apathy as the most pressing problems.

MOTIVATING THE TEACHING STAFF

> Individual counseling sessions with John revealed that he found "school boring" and his "teachers a pain."
> 11/20/82
> John was absent from school between 11/1/82 and 11/15/82. A conference was arranged with John and his mother. Mrs. D. complained that "teachers have never understood John and maybe it is time he dropped out and went to work." She was openly hostile, pointing out that she had five children and couldn't be "running up to school constantly."

KEY ISSUES

A. Can schools identify, prescribe for and assist potential dropouts so that they may gain satisfaction and success in schools as they currently exist?

B. Can faculty, counselors, and administrators develop new strategies to aid marginal students?

C. What steps can be taken by the principal to reassess the learning environment and to initiate changes designed to meet individual students' needs?

D. Can group instruction and a single teaching strategy reach and motivate marginal students?

ANALYSIS: (Proposal Continued)

> The school counselor can serve in a pivotal role in cases like John D.'s. Diagnosis is an important counseling function and is defined as a summary of the student's problems and their causes, a descripton of the individual's personality and an understanding of the way an individual learns best. A thorough knowledge of the student's individual learning style could facilitate the diagnostic process in counseling. The Learning Style Inventory (Dunn, Dunn and Price, 1978) has been used extensively to diagnose students' learning styles and then to prescribe curricular learning interventions to respond to individual needs.
>
> A summary of John D.'s Learning Style Inventory Profile indicates the following:
> - Need for a quiet learning environment
> - Requires bright light

- Prefers warm environment
- Low level of motivation
- Low indication of persistence and responsibility
- Need for structured learning
- Prefers learning with peers
- Tactual and kinesthetic preferences
- Functions best in the afternoon

As counselors, we should share these identified learning style characteristics with John's classroom teachers and assist them to identify instructional resources that are responsive to his needs. The faculty should be encouraged to individualize instruction for those students who cannot function successfully without that specialized attention. The following steps would be suggested for serving marginal students:

1. Administer the <u>Learning Style Inventory</u> to all students with academic problems and develop group profiles based upon environmental (sound, light, temperature, design), emotional (motivation, persistence, responsibility, structure), sociological (peers, self, pair, team, adult, varied), physical (perceptual strengths, intake, time, mobility), and psychological (global/analytic, hemispheric dominance and impulsivity/reflective) characteristics.
2. Redesign the instructional environment by changing the traditional classroom of desks and chairs into a varied learning environment that includes individual and group "offices" and dens, multisensory materials, casual carpeted sections and small-group learning areas.
3. Design multisensory instructional resources to include Contract Activity Packages, Programmed Learning Sequences, Multisensory Instructional Packages and tactual/kinesthetic materials based on interests and related to the curriculum.
4. Match individual learning style characteristics with complementary teaching styles, instructional programs, methods and resources.
5. Monitor the progress of each student individually in terms of the achievement of assigned competencies and selected instructional objectives.

The role of the principal in helping the faculty move from conventional, large group instruction to small group and individualized programs is critical. The principal should distribute to the faculty excerpts of the research which clearly indicates that compatibility between methodology and learning style results in significantly greater student achievement than when students and methods are mismatched. Finally, in-service workshops should be provided to assist the faculty in diagnosing individual learning styles and developing resources and strategies that respond to the diversity of characteristics found among students in each classroom—particularly among marginal students.

Mr. Sage, the principal, read the report twice and was impressed. He put it down and walked through the halls of Grant High. He considered what had been "reality" to date:

"The basic approach at our school, as in most, is group instruction—groups of students are taught by a particular teacher for short periods of time. Certainly, a teacher's instructional methods must be favorable to some students and unfavorable to others. And yet, if there is a consistent mismatch between student and teacher, the student surely must begin to feel inadequate as a learner. That's all that's needed to decrease motivation! From then on, it's downhill!

"Why do we often accept poor grades from certain students rather than working furiously to remediate them? Once our kids have been labeled as 'low achievers,' they develop deviant behavior, cut classes and become aggressive. We ought to develop different kinds of educational environments where youngsters can learn and work toward specific goals through their own learning styles!"

"I'm going to do it," he said aloud. "I'm going to accept the Guidance Department's recommendations and ask for volunteers to work on their proposal."

GUIDELINES

1. Diagnose all students, but focus on their marginal achievers and those identified as potential dropouts, for their ability levels, knowledge, interests and learning styles.
2. Prescribe individual educational plans for such students through the structure of a Child Study Team consisting of staff that have some knowledge of the individual student; e.g., classroom teacher(s), guidance counselor, psychologist, social worker, administrator, aide, and, when appropriate, parent(s) or guardian(s).

3. Design varied programs and train faculty to use appropriate instructional strategies to meet individual student needs.
4. Match students as closely as possible to appropriate teaching styles and programs until a full proposal is implemented.

SITUATION 27

PROBLEM: Overcoming Union Manipulation and Pressures

SITUATION: Case Study

by
Gene Geisert

BACKGROUND

The leadership of the Teachers' Union is preparing secretly to initiate a confrontation over a school principal's right to evaluate classroom teachers. The chief negotiator for the Union plans to present a demand limiting management prerogatives in this area. The plan is to be put into effect at a forthcoming negotiation session. As part of the overall Union strategy to weaken management's position at the bargaining table, the Union president plans to "set up" a grievance action and has targeted a school where the Teacher Building Committee is strongest.

CASE STUDY

Jim Righteous has been a junior high school principal for eight years. Three years ago, the Board of Education granted collective bargaining rights to the teachers, and Jim has, for the past two years, been struggling to understand the new contract and the aggressive independence displayed by some of his staff. The easygoing informal atmosphere that Jim preferred to utilize in working with faculty has given way to more formalized relationships that Jim strongly believes have operated to the detriment of many. One management area that Jim feels has been preserved and reserved to management is staff evaluation. He is reinforced in this belief by the contract clause which states: "The Parties agree that the primary objective of the program to evaluate classroom teaching is to improve the quality of instruction. The Principal shall be responsible for the administration of that process."

He was, therefore, distinctly upset when he was advised by the Union Building Committee that he must give advance notice to any teacher before attempting either a formal or informal observation of the teacher's performance in the classroom.

At first, Jim reverted to his personal style of leadership and verbally agreed to inform each teacher a day or so before he might be observing.

On one occasion last week however, Jim found himself with an unexpected block of free time, and he used the opportunity to visit several teachers unannounced; one of them was on the Union Building Committee.

A grievance was filed immediately, and, as management's front line representative, Jim was required to answer for his alleged improper actions. He was confused initially and unsure of himself. He called the Union president to ask why he was being grieved against. The president told him not to worry and suggested that Jim state that, while he had in the past given everyone prior notice, he slipped up this *one* time and would agree to revert to his past practice of informing teachers of an impending observation before visiting them. If Jim would so respond, the Union president informed him that the Union would withdraw its grievance.

Jim did not have any desire to be "spotlighted" by the Board and superintendent as one of those administrators who is unable to work with staff and felt that a grievance against him might reflect negatively on his record.

KEY ISSUES

    A. Can the principal resort to former patterns of leadership when the "followers" change the organizational climate

through negotiation or strategic, behind-the-scenes planning?
B. Should the principal make decisions without assistance, in a vacuum of knowledge about the issues, the facts and the planned strategy of both sides?
C. Can a middle manager such as a principal work effectively with teachers who are determined to make Union goals their primary professional objective?
D. How can a principal align himself/herself with management and simultaneously maintain an effective professional team relationship with staff?

ANALYSIS

Jim was tempted to capitulate to the Union request that he admit that he had "slipped" this one time after having given prior notice about forthcoming observations. After all, it didn't seem to be much of a demand, and that way there would be no grievance, and the superintendent and Board would not even realize that a grievance had, in fact, been initiated.

The principal's moment of weakness vanished as quickly as it had developed. He knew what the teachers' contract stated about evaluation; it was a critical prerogative of building administrators.

Furthermore, the entire Union approach on this issue began to resemble a predetermined plan—a staged effort designed to establish a procedure that could endanger the very right protected by negotiated agreement.

Jim called the superintendent, brought him up-to-date on the situation, and, with the chief executive's approval, summoned the Union representative into his office and informed him that there was no merit to the Union claim that the negotiated agreement's evaluation clause had been violated. He also stated that he did not agree that not announcing visits to classrooms could be challenged.

GUIDELINES

1. Be certain of the overall management strategy before responding to any grievance. Call or meet with the superintendent or the assistant superintendent for personnel before taking any action.

2. Consider yourself as part of the Management Team and support its efforts to protect and retain its prerogatives.
3. Seek new patterns of effective leadership without reducing your role or changing your values or professional goals. The majority of any staff responds to caring, support and motivation derived from success and accomplishment on the job itself.

SITUATION 28

PROBLEM: Preventing and Overcoming Burnout

SITUATION: Interview

---

by
William Sanders

"Bob, you're the principal! Help us to understand and overcome teacher burnout."

"How do you define burnout?"

"It's a feeling of 'Why continue? What sense is there in going on?' I've developed good motivational techniques and made the information interesting, but by 8th grade they still can't find the city they live in on a map or explain what the United States is. Brooklyn is an unknown—even after I told them in September and again in June; they still don't know! Knowledge that I, as a teacher, try to get across, doesn't seem to have any meaningful impact on my kids' lives; there's no application for them. They're turned on to everything other than the State curriculum!"

"What do you think *causes* burnout?"

"Well, I mentioned the lack of student receptivity. There's also another problem. From a work point of view for teachers, only lateral movement seems to occur. We move from one program to another to another and have the same responsibility and the same accountability. A Reading Program changes and is called "The Academy," and we adapt it for different kinds of kids and work hard at it; and then it's changed again, and we redesign our lessons; and then something new is thrust on us ... but it's only another version of the original reading program. It's always more work, but there's no recognition by the administration, and it's always back to square one."

"When does burnout occur?"

"When you realize how caught you are. You see lack of movement and little response from the kids, and then it starts. It happened to me after five years, and, believe it or not, I've been teaching for fourteen."

"What are the symptoms or tell-tale signs?"

"You don't smile; you don't get involved; you don't volunteer. I used to be Chapter Chairman—now I don't even attend Union meetings. I don't socialize with other faculty members because if we're together, we mostly gripe about the job."

"How could burnout be avoided?"

"Start with the kids. We have to feel we're getting something back from them. While we get the kids psyched up, there are vandals working on our cars. I've been robbed six times myself! I've seen assaults on my friends and had to go to their aid. When it got really bad because of high school kids who were hanging around in the school yard and selling drugs, the building doors were locked, but then the fire department and maintenance said "no." Now, although there are aides at every door, some kids still won't go outside the classroom."

"What about rewards?"

"What rewards? There's no bonus pay. With our kind of institutional bureaucracy, there's no way to get a reward. Although you know you're better than a lot of people in the system, you get the same salary increases that they do each year. There are no standards for kids. Parents don't cooperate. If kids want to go out at night, parents don't say 'no.' A breakdown of family structure is eventually reflected in school breakdown."

"Do you have any suggestions for improving the school system?"

"The problem is twofold: kids and administration. If even only one got better, it would help. There are twelve hundred 7th and 8th graders; small class sizes would help. Middle class parents might help, too, because of their values. But an original faculty of 135 reduced now to 72 veterans who view everything as the same old stuff helps to promote burnout in all of us."

KEY ISSUES

- A. What responsibility does the principal have in recognizing and aiding victims of teacher burnout?
- B. How can a principal prevent burnout?
- C. To what degree is a principal responsible for burnout?
- D. What should a principal do to create school climate, student and teacher positive self-concept and community support in the battle against burnout?

ANALYSIS

Causes

Teacher burnout, a rapidly increasing problem among today's educators, is a result of frustration and the day-to-day stress of waging battle. The battle is on a field of student apathy, absenteeism, drug problems and vandalism, further complicated by a lack of administrative guidance and community support. The joy of teaching begins to disappear and the symptoms are sleeplessness, continual tiredness, the inability to throw off colds, depression, an abnormal desire for vacations and low self-esteem. A feeling of guilt may accompany the helplessness as the teacher gradually surrenders and becomes passive in the system. There seems to be little correlation between self-reported teacher stress and biographical characteristics such as sex, age and length of teaching. Teachers recount that the most common symptoms experienced are those of exhaustion and frustration. However, a survey conducted by the New York State United Teachers of their membership indicated that urban teachers are experiencing a greater degree of stress than rural or suburban teachers and that younger teachers are more susceptible than the experienced. Incompetent administrators and disruptive students were listed as the major causes of such reactions. Some teachers are so affected that they leave the profession. Others hang on and count the days until each vacation or eventual retirement.

Those who stay in this condition withdraw further from their classes; the students become aware of the problem, and this presages more trouble for all concerned.

A large part of the difficulty may be due to inadequate professional training in that teachers have not been taught how to cope with stress. Inept organizational structures have compounded the problem because they often do not provide the authoritative approval that many teachers frequently need.

Prevention

As an action rather than a reaction, one way of preventing burnout would be through college teacher preparatory programs. Coping skills should become part of their curriculum and an ongoing need for a support system could be provided by workshops that focus on the identification of potentially stressful situations and strategies for coping with them.

The first step in stress management is to develop self-awareness; the next is to identify the conditions that cause stress; the third is to learn how to reduce them; a fourth step in any program for dealing with stress should be to prevent development of feelings of isolation. Teachers can be shown that they are not alone; many of their co-workers may share their same concerns. The fifth step would be to examine success stories, to find out where others have encountered burnout symptoms and how they managed to overcome them and to become excited again about teaching. The final step is your own plan of action—a positive, active formula that produces positive change.

The willingness to bring about change, to try a different strategy or tactic, and to design an alternate plan is what counts in the attack on disillusion and frustration. Teachers should be encouraged to design a new curriculum, experiment with a different grade level or a related, but new, subject area, or create new strategies for the part of their teaching that can be altered. They should vary the way they handle discipline problems until they find one way that seems to work better than the others. They need to borrow ideas from successful and respected colleagues.

Encourage the staff to find something that interests them outside of school. Suggest that they join an exercise club, take a film course, try their hand at interior decorating, Japanese cooking, or wine tasting. If they take a day to do only things for themselves, they'll bring it back to the classroom in the form of revitalization.

Principals should involve teachers directly in helping individual students with special problems. Give them the recognition that will increase their self-concept and coping ability. Personal growth, variety and constructive challenge are essential to diminish burnout.

GUIDELINES

1. Be sensitive to continuing high levels of frustration apparently caused by day-to-day lack of success with students, community apathy and destructive behaviors.
2. Provide meetings, workshops and programs to build coping skills and opportunities for recognition, satisfaction, motivation and positive self-concept.
3. Increase your own competence to counsel teachers and students to overcome negative attitudes toward school and learning.
4. Become expert about how students learn and about what will motivate them toward growth and positive self-image. Get them involved constructively in helping themselves to improve academically and to contribute to their respective communities.

SITUATION 29

PROBLEM: Improving an Individual Teacher's Performance

SITUATION: Teachers' Room Complaints

by
Jean Hazelton

Whispered rumors about an inexperienced, nontenured teacher recently were raised to the level of direct complaint and concern by others. As principal, I was surprised to hear of so many directly focused, negative comments from colleagues, students, parents and even special teachers. There were reports of boring, unmotivating classes and a flurry of phone calls from parents requesting meetings to discuss their youngsters' progress. Apparently they already had met with Miss Kaye but felt that matters had been unresolved. Some complained about the educational jargon in her responses.

I usually allow a few weeks of settling in before I visit classrooms, but only two weeks after the beginning of the term I knew it was necessary to arrange to spend time in Miss Kaye's classroom. I brought along the new district observation form that had been developed and approved by a committee of teachers and administrators.

The new observation form was simple when compared with most district checklists, and everyone was convinced that it would be more objective and useful to supervisors and assistants than the old one which required subjective judgments on such items as voice, appearance, cooperation, ethics, and so on. I felt a lot more comfortable using this new instrument with someone who might be having problems than I had with the old one we'd just discarded.

Miss Kaye was a well-groomed, poised, self-confident teacher who greeted me at the classroom door and graciously escorted me to the only vacant chair that just happened to be in the center of the room where I was clearly visible to all the students.

In reviewing her lesson plan, the objectives, the motivational devices and the procedures were all well stated. Technically, all seemed in order—until the lesson began. Within five minutes it became apparent that this teacher was planning to lecture in a monotone for the entire lesson.

The performance was a one-person show with Miss Kaye at the center of the stage and the students seated as the audience—except that they were behaving as if they'd been given half-priced seats. There was little interaction other than the few "Pay attention!" directives that were requested to keep the attention of less tolerant "reviewers." The few questions asked required responses repeating what had been stated by Miss Kaye; nothing that would stimulate critical thinking was introduced. In fact, the questions were almost as dry as the lecture. In no way were students called upon to participate actively either with the teacher or with each other; indeed, they were cautioned to "Sit quietly" and to "Listen!" almost as often as they evidenced their inability to do so.

It goes without saying that there was no evidence that instruction was being adapted to suit individual differences or that the teacher was alert to the physical, emotional, environmental, social or psychological characteristics of individual students. As I examined the room, I saw that the bulletin boards were teacher-made without any student work displayed. The learning climate was sterile and superficial, and it was rather apparent that no more than fifteen to twenty percent of the students were either taking notes or listening attentively.

When dittoed science sheets were distributed, all the students had to solve the same problems in the same period of time. The few who had listened to the lecture and had taken notes seemed to be able to answer most of the questions; on the other hand, more than half the students seemed irritable and restless.

It didn't take a new observation form to verify that Miss Kaye had not analyzed the students' ability levels, interests, learning strengths or styles. Equally obvious was the lack of specific instructional strategies to involve students actively nor did her techniques respond to different learning characteristics.

KEY ISSUES

A. How much credence should a principal give to complaints about a teacher from parents? From other teachers? From students?
B. After thorough screening and cooperative faculty/administrator decisions on the employment of an inexperienced teacher, how should the principal proceed in the development of teaching competence?
C. How can parents and concerned teachers be helped to develop confidence and patience as the principal embarks on the upgrading process?
D. Should a teacher who does not respond and improve within two to three months be retained for the entire year? Two years? More?

ANALYSIS AND SOLUTION

This teacher had a great many strengths which were observed by personnel screening teams and the principal during the interview process. She was very intelligent, knowledgeable in a surprising number of subject areas at the elementary school level and had exhibited a willingness to learn and to work hard.

Unfortunately, her training and background had focused on subject matter almost exclusively. Her recommendations were from college trainers with a similar philosophy. Last, Miss Kaye had done very well academically while in college by listening and taking notes; as with most teachers, she was teaching the way she learned best—not in the way her individual students learned best.

Several approaches were possible, but I decided to enlist the aid of my assistant principal who was a Master Teacher, and who enjoyed giving demonstration lessons on small-group techniques and practical ways to individualize instruction. She and I scheduled a series of meetings with Miss Kaye and reviewed individual students' records; we then discussed ways to develop alternative instructional strategies to respond to different youngsters' learning styles. We also suggested that she read specific articles and books that explained both theory and "how to" approaches.

Miss Kaye, who was understandably upset at first, asked for time to see effective teachers in action and to have the assistant principal assist her with classroom management when she began using the new instructional techniques. A slightly depressed Miss Kaye eventually bubbled with enthusiasm when the matching of teaching strategies with students' abilities, interests and learning styles began to produce increased academic achievement and improved attitudes toward school.

Several veteran teachers and the assistant principal agreed to help Miss Kaye develop multisensory resources for the new approaches and some room redesigns to support the emerging plans. Between us, the assistant principal and I visited her class at least twice a week and held almost daily meetings with Miss Kaye for the next two months. We were delighted with the progress she made. In particular, she evidenced a budding, artistic talent for creating tactual and kinesthetic materials for students who had difficulty listening or reading. In fact, some of the other teachers asked if they could copy those new resources for use with their inattentive, non-listening youngsters.

GUIDELINES

1. The principal must be aware of the instructional ability of each of his teachers at all times. Teachers new to a building should receive early observation and supervision.
2. When problems arise, an assessment should be made immediately concerning the nature of the teaching deficit(s) or ineffective instructional approach(es) and a plan for improvement should be designed and implemented as soon as possible.

3. The concerned teacher and those supervisors and other teachers who can provide a support and amelioration system should be part of the planning-for-improvement process.
4. Continuing follow-up observations and assistance must be scheduled on a regular basis.
5. Observation forms and procedures should be objective and should relate directly to the improvement of instruction. They should assess the existence of: (a) clearly written objectives by the teacher and suggestions for how they are to be addressed by youngsters of differing ability levels; (b) instructional strategies and procedures that are appropriate for different learning styles and can be observed by the supervisor; (c) learning outcomes that are visible in the instructional environment because of the planning and actions of teachers and students; and (d) pre- and posttest achievement scores to verify each student's progress in relation to his/her baseline data.

SITUATION 30

PROBLEM: Dealing with Low Teacher Morale

SITUATION: Informal Meeting

by
Joseph M. Aquino and Erika Wick

As principal of Hillside High School, Dr. David Kamm was mindful of the deleterious effect that an impersonal note could have when placed in a teacher's mailbox—particularly when it requested a meeting with the principal. Consequently, whenever it was possible, he was certain to schedule such a meeting verbally. He knew that Peter Evans, a twelve-year veteran social studies teacher, had a preparation period during the first period of the school day; thus, Dr. Kamm waited near the teachers' mailboxes before classes began. As Dr. Kamm greeted some of the teachers, he saw Mr. Evans heading for his box. Smiling as he approached, Dr. Kamm said, "Good morning, Pete. May I see you for a minute?"

Mr. Evans responded, "Sure, Dave." The two men then walked toward the door marked, "Dr. David Kamm, Principal," and entered the room. As they sat down, Mr. Evans said, "What's the problem, Dave?"

Leaning forward in his chair, Dr. Kamm, a benign but serious expression on his face said, "I'm concerned about you lately, Pete. You seem to have lost the infectious spark that used to characterize your interaction with your students and colleagues. It's as though you're going through the motions rather than giving your all, and you know how important a teacher's attitude toward his students is. It's half the battle of motivating them. That's why I'm concerned. Is anything wrong?—and if so, can I help?"

Pete Evans sat there, absorbing what he'd heard and considering his answer. After a few moments he said, "Dave, things have changed here. The sole purpose of the present Board of Education seems to be to squeeze every extra ounce of bureaucratic paper work they can out of us. The parents act as though our job is to give their children good grades so they'll be accepted at fine colleges. And the students don't respect us because we have no control over this situation. I became a teacher because I believed in the goals of good education, but how can anyone maintain his 'spark' under these circumstances?"

A bit surprised at the nature of the reply, Dr. Kamm looked at the stack of work on his desk and then at Mr. Evans and said, "Pete, I agree that education is not in a priority position in the minds of most people and that the economic and cultural changes we are witnessing are reflected in the things you've spoken of, but we have a duty to perform to the best of our abilities, and that is to provide the best possible education we can. Our students did not create these circumstances, and perhaps many of them are too immature to understand the very real and personal value of a good education. However, they deserve one, and you know whether or not you've done your job well. If you have, your colleagues will appreciate it and respect you for it, and more important, you'll know you've done your best and as a result, enjoy your work. Perhaps when they grow older, your former students will occasionally remember your influence, too. You're a very creative teacher, and your students and this school can benefit from the use of your full capability."

The two men rose from their seats, and as they walked to the door, Dr. Kamm said, "Pete, you have my support, and if there's anything I can do to make a tough but important job easier, please ask."

Pete responded, "Thanks, that's good to know," and left the room. Dr. Kamm returned to his desk, hoping that his words had added a modicum of inspiration for continued investment in the students.

Dr. Kamm knew that Mr. Evans' contentions about the current condition of education at Hillside High School were valid. He, too, had seen the public's views of education change; he had been involved in the profession for nearly thirty years. He'd watched a decline in respect for the importance of the task; he'd seen the economic difficulties of the society reflected in the Board's efforts to get more for its money; and he'd observed students doing things they wouldn't have dared do when he'd begun in the profession. Nonetheless, doing his job well meant doing his utmost to keep teacher morale as high as possible. Teachers with low morale didn't necessarily deserve to be fired, but they weren't performing at their highest levels. That meant that the students weren't getting the best education they could, and consequently, the future of education would not improve. He believed that improving teacher morale was an investment in both the present and the future, and he'd acted accordingly.

KEY ISSUES

A. How does a principal observe and discuss conditions causing low morale?
B. What can the leader of a building do to reverse feelings that reduce teaching effectiveness?

ANALYSIS

This case depicts a situation wherein a principal understands the reasons for the low morale of teachers and still attempts to overcome negative attitudes. He places great value on his profession and wisely works at helping the central employee of the school system, the teacher, perform his duties well. He realizes that in educating students, the person who has the most contact with, and consequently the greatest potential influence on them, is the teacher. He is aware that educational systems are often the scapegoat of a society in that they are often the first institutions to feel the onslaught of an economic crunch. He knows that the lack of deference and courtesy toward the professionals in this field affects their interest in their work, and he sympathizes with them. However, he endeavors to help them maintain their conscientiousness.

How can the teacher's morale be improved under these conditions? Dr. Kamm's response suggests an awareness that while he can't change the culture by himself, he can support his faculty and thereby help to create an atmosphere more conducive to relatively high morale. He does this by understanding the situation, by sympathizing with their plight, by complimenting them on their abilities and on jobs done well and by keeping his goal and theirs—good education—in sight. In short, he sets an example of sincerity and interest.

Other actions to influence teachers like Pete could involve attempting to reverse attitudes of students by including them in joint meetings with faculty to plan improvements in the high school. Student and teacher enthusiasm might, in turn, change parents' feelings about the school and raise community morale.

GUIDELINES

1. Stay in personal contact with staff members to determine their consistent moods, attitudes and morale as they affect performance.
2. Offer both informal and formal support to improve any situation which may lead to poor morale and lack of enthusiasm for teaching and learning.

7
Managing the Change Process

SITUATION 31

> **PROBLEM:** Upholding Students' Rights and Eliminating Questionable Practices
>
> **SITUATION:** Office Confrontation

by
Patricia A. Green

Kay Martin, a recent transfer student now in the tenth grade, made an appointment to see Dr. Samuel Evans, principal of Middletown High School.

When Kay got to Dr. Evans' office on Monday morning, she was nervous but decided to go through with the meeting anyway.

Dr. Evans asked: "What can I do for you, Kay?"

"Well, Dr. Evans, I don't like to complain, but I just got my first semester grades here at Middletown, and I got a C− in Ms. Wilson's Math class, and I sure didn't deserve it. I'm new to the school, but I did hear the rumors about her unfair grades; I just didn't believe she could be so arbitrary and capricious. More than half the class got Ds and Fs!"

Dr. Evans was aware of the increasing unrest concerning Ms. Wilson's math classes; student enrollment in her groups had been decreasing each semester, and several parents had complained recently about their daughters' grades and the obvious preference Ms. Wilson had for the boys in her classes.

Dr. Evans told Kay he would look into the matter immediately.

He pulled Carol Wilson's file, and at the same time requested Kay Martin's file as well.

During the early years of her twenty-year teaching career at Middletown High School, Carol Wilson's evaluations were good. In more recent years her evaluations could be summarized rather succinctly:

Student Involvement: None

Faculty Relations: None

Extracurricular Activities: None

He called his secretary, and asked her to have Ms. Wilson come to his office before leaving the building that day. At 3:00 p.m., after all the buses had left and the building was quiet, Carol Wilson came into Dr. Evans' office.

She listened quietly as Dr. Evans explained his morning meeting with Kay Martin and the previous conversations that had taken place with the parents of other girls.

When Dr. Evans finished, Carol Wilson responded that she thought there was little to discuss; she was an excellent teacher but a tough marker with very high standards. She had small classes, but that's the way she wanted it; she wasn't in a popularity contest. Having taught in this school for twenty years, she believed she knew exactly what should be done, and excellence was not open to discussion. It was that simple; if students didn't like either her teaching or her grading, they should not sign up for her classes!

She stood up and said she hoped that there would be no more discussion about this nonsense. She was curt, and revealed the same hostility that had manifested itself so many other times in both the faculty room and at faculty meetings.

The meeting was over, but the problem was not.

The next day Kay Martin was summoned to Dr. Evans' office and was told by him in a most friendly matter that he had looked over her transcript from Burr High School and knew that she was an excellent and conscientious student. He saw that she had earned B+s and As in all her courses and told her that he understood her great disappointment in the recent C− in math. However, there was nothing that he could do to intervene, because Ms. Wilson's grades were her decision, and no one could change them. He suggested that Kay make an appointment to speak to Ms. Wilson directly. He concluded by suggesting that she allow one more semester for the period of adjustment to Middletown High School in the hope that she would see things differently. He told her to "have a nice day," as she quietly closed the door behind her.

KEY ISSUES

A. At what point does the protection of academic freedom in grading become a license to abuse the rights of students to careful, objective and fair marks based on performance and relative standing regardless of sex, personality and possible prejudice?

B. How does a principal support a range of academic freedoms that are appropriate and at the same time demand equitable, professional judgments on grades and student assessments?

C. To what extent and with what response does a principal use student and parent feedback in either improving grading practices or in other situations?

ANALYSIS

The principal must contend with each teacher who alienates many students, regardless of whether that person is newly appointed or tenured. When a faculty member grades harshly, discourages students from signing up for his/her classes, promotes a negative reputation, reveals bias or favoritism and/or is hostile or uncooperative with either youngsters or colleagues, it is the principal's responsibility to intervene and provide guidance. In this case, the teacher was also either oblivious to, or unconcerned about, the "instructional leader's" intervention in the matter; she maintained sole jurisdiction and permitted neither discussion nor recommendations. The principal's leadership role was completely obviated. Because of his strong belief in academic freedom, and despite knowledge of the difficulty in bringing charges against tenured faculty, the principal should have begun to document evidence bearing on the fairness, objectivity and potential prejudice of this teacher when the first parents' complaints were brought to his attention. Charts containing courses taught, enrollment, patterns of grades over the years, grades given to boys and girls, comparisons with the majority of grades given to similar students by other instructors who have taught the same courses, grades obtained by students in other math courses and their overall academic performance and potential should have been prepared by the department chairperson.

Meetings with the chairperson, the teacher concerned and the principal then should have been held to discuss the data objectively. Should no improvement have resulted, written instructions from the principal should have explicitly required objectivity; follow-up memoranda should have been forwarded if the pattern continued.

Charges, hearings, a transfer, a suspension and eventual dismissal are potential courses of action if persuasion fails. Although dismissal through tenure hearings in most states is difficult, action must be taken when the rights of one group, the students, are abridged under the guise of another right; in this situation, the academic freedom of teachers to assess performance. The principal must be prepared to uphold students' rights when a faculty member clearly abuses his or her responsibilities and privileges.

GUIDELINES

1. Grades for individual student performance should be based on the achievement of academically assigned goals and scholastic standards that are clearly and accurately communicated to students and parents.
2. Fair and consistent grading should be universal throughout the building and district.
3. A *minimum* class size should be set, below which a class will *not* run for that semester. Class size, both for required and elective courses, should be established by a joint committee of faculty and administrators, recommended by the Superintendent of Schools and approved by the Board of Education.
4. Department chairpersons should be authorized to review grading patterns, teaching procedures and test development under the supervision of the principal.
5. Team teaching, peer evaluation and student evaluation of staff should be considered in certain situations.

SITUATION 32

> **PROBLEM:** Planning Time and Priorities: How to Close an Always Open Door
>
> **SITUATION:** An Urgent Note

by
Erika Wick and Joseph M. Aquino

Dr. Diana Henderson assumed the principalship of Lincoln High School when Bill Jacobs retired a little more than a year before. Bill had been a popular principal whose door was always open to anybody. His critics, however, maintained that he was more interested in keeping his staff happy than in getting the job done. The verifiable fact was that Lincoln High's students scored close to the bottom in reading, writing and mathematics skills when compared with students from other, similar public high schools.

When Diana took over, she set a thirty percent scholastic improvement goal to be achieved within five years. To reach that objective she had to mobilize teachers and parents, gain the cooperation of the Board of Education and obtain funds for special services. That task required extensive time and effort, and because Diana was most productive when not interrupted, she changed her predecessor's always-open-door-policy. Her office hours were posted as 8:30–9:30 A.M., and 1:30–2:30 P.M. daily. Anybody could see her during those hours without having to make an appointment. At other times, she was available by appointment and anytime in case of an emergency.

This new policy was not popular with the teachers who were used to having unlimited access to the principal's office. They contended that the new policy would drastically affect teacher morale, because the closed door set principal and teachers apart, stressing an authoritarian, rather than a collegial, relationship and indicated a lack of empathy and understanding. However, when, after one year, students' achievement scores in all areas were up by approximately fifteen percent, and the parents had become much more interested and involved in school concerns, most teachers conceded that Dr. Henderson's productivity-oriented policy was in the school's best interest.

Early in the fall of her second year, after working till nearly 5:00 P.M. one Tuesday, Dr. Henderson handed her secretary a folder of papers. She had just finished filling out the application for a grant that could provide services to help girls overcome math anxiety. Diana thanked her secretary for sparing her any interruptions during that day's closed-door hours. "Please get the application typed and mailed by tomorrow afternoon so that we can meet the deadline," she continued. Dr. Henderson then proceeded to empty the message box and to take her notes to her office.

She glanced through the envelopes and opened the only one that was sealed. The note inside from Sandra Miller caused Diana to mumble, "Again?", as she read the message. Sandra was a "regular" at the principal's office, a friendly teacher who cared about students but who was overwhelmed by discipline problems. For example, the previous week when a boy called her a "fat lump," she was so upset that she had to stay home for a day to recuperate.

Diana read the note again and then called in the secretary. "What did Ms. Miller say when she came to the office today?" "She wanted to see you right away," the secretary reported. "When I told her you were trying to meet a deadline for a grant proposal, she looked very hurt. When I asked whether the meeting was urgent, she said, 'It depends on your viewpoint.' I offered her an appointment for tomorrow, but she declined. Instead, she left a written message for you and requested that I be certain you read it today. She said it was personal, but important."

The principal asked for Ms. Miller's phone number and returned to her office. She called Sandra, and while the phone rang, she read the note over again:

> I have just been informed by my doctor that a bed will be available tomorrow at Clearview Hospital. Since I have to undergo surgery as soon as possible, I request a two- to four-week medical leave. Your "Closed Door" policy made it impossible for me to tell you in person.

Sandra Miller answered the phone's first ring, and Diana apologized for not having seen her. She asked about Sandra's condition and about her need for surgery. The principal also wanted to know why Sandra had not *insisted* on a meeting, considering the importance of the matter. Ms. Miller explained that she preferred not to mention the need for hospitalization to the secretary because she didn't care to respond to additional questions. She didn't want anyone to know the reason for her request. "Can you imagine what the students would call me if they found out about my mastectomy? I could never teach at Lincoln High again!"

Two weeks later, the superintendent asked Dr. Henderson whether it was true that she had made access to her office so difficult that a teacher could not even tell her about an emergency hospitalization.

KEY ISSUES

A. Should a principal's door be open to staff at all times? Each principal must determine the extent to which he/she wishes to adhere to either an open or closed-door policy. Either position has both merits and problems.

The *Always Open Door* invites friendliness, cooperation and a sense of interaction and power-sharing; but it denies the principal the opportunity to schedule desk work constructively and to count on uninterrupted, productive time.

The *Always Closed Door* gives the principal total control over access to his/her office, and, thus, time can be allocated productively. Appointments can be responsive to the workload, and interruptions either can be minimized or eliminated; unnecessary meetings are discouraged. Although the principal's productivity ultimately benefits the school, those who wish to confer may view the policy as a symbolic representation of the principal's lack of interest in their work or an absence of human concern. They may feel frustrated by a sense of powerlessness as they wait to find out when their meetings will take place. Staff and community alienation could offset the principal's personal productivity record and leave the school without appropriate gains.

B. Can an effective compromise be achieved? Ideally, a conciliatory position would permit office accessibility according to the needs of a given faculty and the principal's individual productivity style. Solutions for exceptional situations could be outlined in the established procedures. A principal's demonstrated cooperative manner should balance any inconveniences the staff experiences because of limited access time.

C. *Reevaluations of a Policy.* New policies should be periodically reevaluated for their efficiency. Successes as well as failures have to be studied and their origins traced. Both positive and negative outcomes can be taken into account only if they are a direct result of the established system. Secondary results from causes unrelated to the policy should not influence policy evaluation.

ANALYSIS

When the superintendent asked about Dr. Henderson's office access policy, especially as it pertained to Sandra Miller's case, the principal of Lincoln High School was afforded an opportunity to present her own analysis:

1. Her predecessor's always-open-door policy had been changed to an open-door policy restricted to two hours a day and for emergencies that were labeled as such. The new policy had not changed the principal's actual conference time; it merely modified the access policy. Two hours each day had adequately served the demonstrated needs.

2. The modified access policy consolidated the unrestricted office access time to the predictable two hours daily, while unpredictable demand for time fragments scattered throughout the day might have interrupted the principal's work at crucial moments. The intrusion-free working hours had increased the principal's productivity which was reflected in accomplishments such as the fifteen percent increase in student achievement. Better cooperation had been obtained from parents and from the Board of Education. Grant money had been received to reduce students' reading problems. Teacher morale was up from last year, as the staff had begun to consider itself a winning team.

3. The teachers' loss of immediate access to power was balanced by an always-open-door policy in case of an emergency. This powersharing gesture expressed the principal's respect for the judgment of those who wanted to see her. It gave the staff the responsibility for, as well as the power of, unlimited access to her office, providing that the password "emergency" was used.

4. Teachers' *fears* that a principal's increased ambitions for a school was equated with *decreased human concern* for teachers, students and parents had played a part in the teacher resistance to the open-door policy change. The principal's record of demonstrated interest in human issues and her acclaimed ability to communicate had dispelled all such concerns until the poorly reported case of Sandra Miller cast doubt, especially because it did involve a case of emergency.

5. The case of Sandra Miller had to be considered an *exception*. Ms. Miller's case was an emergency. Although in possession of the password to the principal's office, Sandra chose, for whatever reason (lack of assertiveness, difficulty in logical thinking under pressure, game-playing, and so on) to make use of it by not reporting the situation accordingly. That choice was Sandra's; it was beyond the principal's control and outside the realm of her responsibility. Neither the policy nor the principal can be blamed for the unfortunate event, since the problem in this case was not with the system but with Ms. Miller herself.

6. No system is *one hundred percent* fail-safe. Systems are expected to work under normal circumstances. Variables unrelated to policy issues cannot be introduced to serve as causes for changing an effective system.

The superintendent and Dr. Henderson agreed that the principal's modified open-door policy worked well for:

a. the principal's productivity;
b. overall school achievements; and
c. serious seekers of access to the principal.

They concluded that therefore the modified open-door policy should remain in effect.

GUIDELINES

1. Staff should have access to the principal in a variety of ways, both formal and informal. Formal meetings should be scheduled and organized for timeliness and effectiveness in reaching goals, solving problems, completing tasks and planning.

2. The principal's needs to complete work and deal with problems and plans should be accommodated through the scheduling of uninterrupted time.
  3. Accessibility during emergencies or crises should be immediate and the one exception to the closed-door.

SITUATION 33

> **PROBLEM:** Using Regional Accreditation to Design Teams at the Top
>
> **SITUATION:** Department Chairperson Unrest

by
Shirley A. Griggs

The Department Chairpersons had an unusual meeting at a restaurant out of town. They sat in the rear of the lounge and consumed far more beer and pretzels than was their custom.

Their unhappiness was directed at the superintendent, not the principal whom they liked and respected, even if they didn't always agree with him.

They kept reading the superintendent's News Release:

> For the third time in three decades our high school is undergoing an internal self-examination. This two-year procedure is required for reaccreditation by the Middle States Association of Colleges and Schools ...

What really upset them was the way the superintendent interfered in their area of responsibility and seemed to take full credit for anything good that happened. Worse than that, he had been criticizing the high school publicly and in a pattern that was hardly constructive.

Their key role in improving their departments and in working with the principal to maintain and raise standards had been ignored by the superintendent. He had sent his assistant to the high school on an almost daily mission to identify "areas in need of improvement" and to give direction to the principal and the staff. Some of this activity seemed to be a result of the gripes of only a few parents.

Now that the accreditation process was facing them, they knew that they'd have to carry the bulk of the load, and, simultaneously, they'd been stripped of leadership. They also perceived themselves as being under fire by a chief executive who never visited the school but had made many judgments about it. They decided to meet with the principal on Monday.

KEY ISSUES

1. Should schools invest the considerable effort necessary for a successful accreditation process?
2. What role should central office staff play in the accreditation process?
3. How can the principal maintain control of processes that fall under his/her jurisdiction?
4. How can the principal share leadership with key professional staff members?

ANALYSIS

Some principals view accreditation with skepticism and maintain that regional accreditation is no longer as important as it once was. Initially, accreditation was developed as a means of facilitating the admission of students to college and as a process for improving articulation between secondary schools and institutions of higher education. Additionally, accreditation was developed so that better schools could identify themselves publicly and protect themselves collectively against competitors who claimed quality without evaluation. It has been argued that these factors are no longer important; admission to college is now dependent much more on a student's scores on objective tests and other factors than on the accredited status of the school from which the student is graduated.

Other building administrators believe that the accreditation standards do not allow for flexibility, innovation or the special needs of specialized schools. They argue that no single set of requirements can serve well the diversity of secondary schools. Moreover, the extension of accreditation to elementary, middle and junior high schools should not consist chiefly of modifying and applying existing accreditation policies and practices to those institutions.

In spite of such criticisms, the advantages of seeking regional accreditation often seem to far outweigh the limitations. Principals acknowledge that the process brings recognition to member schools, encourages the achievement of higher standards, attains status for all involved, builds public confidence and, through self-examination, tends to improve the quality of staff and administrative performance. When striving for accreditation, the entire staff of a school is obliged to formulate cooperatively a specifically detailed statement of purpose regarding the existence of the school. The process itself mandates continual self-study and improvement toward maximizing educational effectiveness. Institutions that fail to provide for their own self-renewal stagnate and eventually lose sight of their purpose and objectives.

A cohesive team approach at the building level is necessary if the high school is to be evaluated fairly. The principal should make the superintendent and central office executives aware of the needs of the staff at this critical time. A high school undergoing an evaluation should receive support and encouragement during the entire accreditation process.

In addition to meeting with the superintendent and other central office personnel, the principal should assume a leadership role in the accreditation process. He or she should:

1. Contact the appropriate agency and obtain the latest "Standards and Procedures for Accrediting Schools" for the level of school involved.

2. Communicate the standards to staff, central office, Board of Education and the community. Those generally include "Philosophy and Objectives, Program of Studies, Guidance Services, Library, School Staff, Records, Administration, Plant and Equipment,

School and Community Relations, Financial Support and School Atmosphere."

3. Organize the school faculty, students, staff, parents and community to prepare for accreditation. The process of preparing for accreditation needs to be collaborative and task-oriented. The school principal must be committed to the process of evaluation and not merely responsive to an external agency. The enthusiasm of the top school administrator for the opportunity to engage in the self-study process must be conveyed throughout the school and community. Tasks that need to be accomplished include the following:

- Select a person to direct the self-study and to have ultimate responsibility for the written report. This person is usually a school administrator (assistant principal, department chairperson or supervisor), with strong leadership qualities and knowledge concerning faculty competencies and skills.
- Appoint a central steering committee to work with the director to clarify goals and objectives that should be pyramidal in structure and include three general levels (Iwanicki, 1976)[1] as follows:

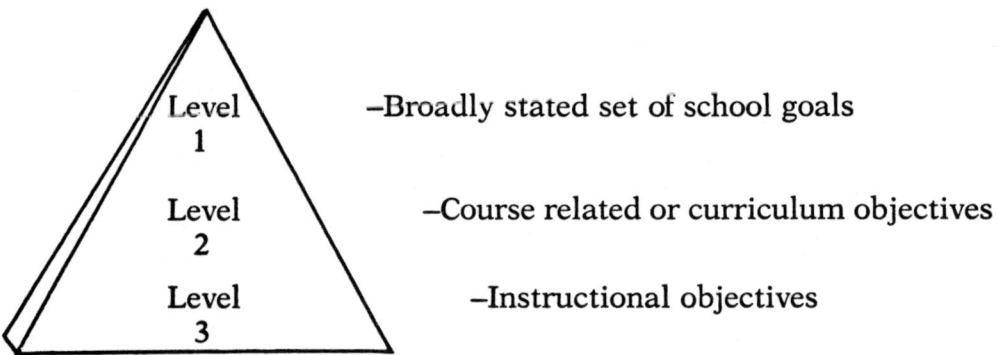

The central steering committee can become a "team at the top". Department chairpersons and key faculty members can be given responsibility and authority for initiating and conducting the evaluative process. That group can involve other faculty and staff in the development of the written assessment report.

---

[1] Iwanicki, Edward F., Developing a secondary school evaluation program. *National Association of Secondary School Principals Bulletin*, 60, 1976, 71-76.

- Keep students, parents and the community informed concerning the accreditation process through press releases.

4. Prepare for the on-site visit by the representatives of the accrediting agency. The school is generally responsible for securing accommodations for the ten to fifteen members of the accrediting team. An agenda needs to be prepared for their two or three-day visit and should include an orientation to the school and community, meetings with various personnel, visits to classes, examinations of records and test data and a sharing of observations and findings with appropriate faculty or departments.

5. Utilize the accreditation results. The report from the accrediting agency, in addition to providing a rating that either accredits or does not accredit the school, contains sections on "strengths, limitations or weaknesses, and recommendations." A definite plan for the use of those results needs to be developed, with careful attention to the recommendations. Since reaccreditation occurs approximately every decade, provisions need to be made to ensure ongoing evaluation and follow-up.

GUIDELINES

1. Regional accreditation offers an official framework for self-evaluation and follow-up improvement. It is well worth the investment of principal and staff time and effort.
2. Seek to obtain Central Office support and encouragement.
3. Maintain control of the entire process through communication and direct involvement.
4. Establish a "team at the top" with a director and key personnel who are given authority and responsibility for the process.

SITUATION 34

> PROBLEM: Visiting Classrooms Is Only Part of Supervision
>
> SITUATION: Student Appeal

*by
Kathy Shanahan*

After the first two months of school, a small group of eighth grade students expressed their concerns about Mr. Simpson, the science teacher. They complained to their homeroom teacher, Miss Bradly, that groups were self-selected and that classwork and lab reports were being completed by one or two members and then copied by the others. Excessive cheating was going on during tests, and constant, disruptive behavior was making it impossible to learn. The frustrated students suggested that unfair advantage was being taken of Mr. Simpson because he was new to the school.

Miss Bradly, who was Teacher-Coordinator of the seventh and eighth grades, suggested that the group make an initial appointment with Mr. Simpson and then with the principal to discuss the situation. The students elected to go directly to the principal, Ms. Robertson, because they had spoken to Mr. Simpson without effect.

Ms. Robertson listened carefully and promised to be more visible during their science classes. She would observe the situation by sitting in on the class and participating in whatever activity was introduced.

Two weeks passed, and the concerned group reported progress to Miss Bradly. The class functioned in an orderly, busy fashion when Ms. Robertson was present. However, once the principal was out of sight, chaos returned.

During parent-teacher conferences, several parents expressed their disapproval of Mr. Simpson's inability to control his class. Parents of students with behavior problems demanded a seating arrangement that would separate cliques. Trouble that began in his chaotic classroom carried over into the halls. Parents were aware that science marks were unusually high and inconsistent with other achievement levels. Ms. Robertson was astounded, because parent disapproval concerning any school matter had seldom been verbalized in the past. She promised to give the matter immediate attention. She discussed the problem with Miss Bradly in the cafeteria during lunch.

Ms. Robertson: Do you know that the situation in Simpson's class hasn't improved?

Miss Bradly: Yes, students and some parents have brought it to my attention.

Ms. Robertson: Parents are really perturbed. I guess I should speak to Simpson—unless you would rather do it.

Miss Bradly: I really don't feel that I'm in a position to do that. Even though I'm the Coordinator, that is not in my jurisdiction.

Ms. Robertson: You know how I feel about interfering with a teacher's right to conduct a class in a manner in which he feels most comfortable.

Miss Bradly: Academic freedom is something that most of the teachers in this building really appreciate and use wisely. I'm sure John (Simpson) won't feel that he is in jeopardy of losing it if he is approached correctly. Maybe he really wants a little direction but is shy about seeking it since he is new to the staff.

Ms. Robertson: Has he ever asked you for help?

Miss Bradly: Never, even though I have dropped subtle hints by describing my own problems at our level meetings.

Ms. Robertson: Well, I'll think about it carefully before I speak with him.

The confrontation never took place. Parent and student vocalization ceased, but the problem persisted throughout the year. Rude behavior developed into physical actions, and, of course, the students' attitudes were not confined to the boundaries of the science room. Crises developed in other classes, and teachers found themselves resolving situations that didn't pertain to their own subjects. When a difficult situation developed, the principal stalled until it either improved or was forgotten. Ms. Robertson's sole action occurred at graduation. She instructed Mr. Simpson to give the science award to a bright student who she felt was deserving of the recognition rather than the candidate he had selected. Mr. Simpson readily complied.

KEY ISSUES

A. Classroom observation is essential but must be weighed against what occurs when observers are not present.
B. Students have a right to learn in a positive and disciplined classroom atmosphere.
C. A principal must be aware of what is happening in all classrooms and take appropriate supervisory actions.

Unless the principal is a "shut-in," he or she would have to be aware of the everyday occurrences in the school. If inappropriate daily events are repeated, thus forming a negative pattern, the principal must have knowledge of the situation. If those conditions persist, the principal *must* take action. This principal was aware of the situation even before the students confronted her with the problem, and should have made daily visits to each classroom a priority task. Although the class seemed orderly during her visits, she knew what happened as soon as she left.

Laissez-faire administration was evident. When student and parent pressures subsided, the situation was ignored again. The science teacher had years of teaching experience in that field. Perhaps the principal did not approach him because she felt incompetent confronting an experienced teacher in a subject area in which she had not been trained.

The junior high seventh and eighth grade Coordinator was inappropriately (and unsuccessfully) asked by the principal to act as the instructional supervisor. The Coordinator's responsibility was to plan and schedule classes—not to improve teaching and management techniques in other teachers' classes. Finally, the principal's only direct action in the entire situation was the selection of the recipient of the science award at graduation exercises.

Obviously, this principal developed no working rapport with the new teacher. She did not help him adapt to a new situation, and her refusal to interefere with academic freedom was simply an excuse for not exercising her given supervisory role. Acting out of authority, frustration and noninterference all year, she signaled her displeasure to Mr. Simpson by overruling his choice of a science award recipient. Being laissez-faire when she should have been directive, and being autocratic when she should have been democratic, was ineffective administration.

There are certain crisis situations that require immediate administrative actions; those should be collaborative and evaluative, for they are essential to the proper functioning of a school.

GUIDELINES

1. Administrators should observe classrooms in action, research reports or incidents that are important to the functioning of the school and take collaborative and decisive actions to improve poor or mediocre situations.
2. Administrators should be aware of each other's management methods and periodically discuss their effectiveness and provide positive suggestions and specific assistance.
3. Accountability should be broadened to include control and management in addition to academics.
4. The administrator should clarify for each faculty member specific goals and expectations at the beginning of each year. Conferences should follow to evaluate progress toward those goals on a continuing basis.
5. Each teacher, especially a new faculty member, should be made aware of all school and classroom regulations, procedures and required strategies.
6. Many formal and informal observations of new teachers, followed by discussions and counseling conferences, should be scheduled to assist teachers to improve professionally.

SITUATION 35

PROBLEM: Making the Right Supervisory Decision at the Right Time

SITUATION: Mismatching Teacher and Student

by
Donal F. Buckley

Peter Daly attended Middletown High School and, during his four years there, was an excellent student in every subject except geometry and physics. He was sober about his work, and although he was an oustanding athlete, he and his parents decided that during his first year of high school he would not participate in any extracurricular activities so that he would have sufficient time to study and, thus, do very well academically. At the end of his freshman year, Peter achieved a ninety-five percent average. In his sophomore year, he was doing equally as well in all subjects except geometry, where he was, at best, a "seventy-percent student." Early in the sophomore year, Peter realized that he was going to have difficulty with geometry because of the teaching style of the instructor, Mr. Harry Caputo.

Mr. Caputo was a very firm teacher who generally taught by lecturing; there was little, if any, direct interaction with the students. He was extremely systematic and never changed his approach—even when answering the few questions that were posed by his students. Although Peter asked questions, he could rarely understand Mr. Caputo's responses.

Harry Caputo, in turn, was very concerned about Peter's grades. He offered to tutor Peter and said that he was always available for additional help. Peter did attend tutoring sessions and additional help classes, but his efforts were fruitless; he still could not understand very much that Mr. Caputo explained.

Because the school was small, transferring the youngster to another teacher was impossible. Peter completed geometry with a seventy percent average but had a ninety-four percent average for all other courses.

In his junior year, Peter did not have Harry Caputo as his teacher and completed the semester with a ninety-six percent average. In Peter's senior year he was once again assigned to Mr. Caputo, but this time for physics. At the onset of the course, Peter, his parents, Mr. Caputo and the principal all were well aware of what had happened in Peter's previous geometry classes. All agreed that Peter should take the physics course because he would need it for college; once again, having another teacher was not feasible because only one section of physics was being offered.

Throughout the year, Peter did poorly on the physics examinations and reluctantly sought the additional help which Mr. Caputo freely gave. It should be noted that Harry Caputo was considered an excellent teacher by most, and he was fair and consistent in his grading practices. Many of his students did exceptionally well on Regents examinations.

KEY ISSUES

A. What options are open to an administrator when a mismatched student and teacher are scheduled for classes in which the student will not do well no matter how well-intentioned all involved are?
B. How important is timing in addressing and resolving critical placement issues?
C. Can teaching style be modified in cases of an obvious mismatching of learning style and instructional method?

ANALYSIS

The difficulty in this situation may have been caused by the teacher's traditional and autocratic instructional style. That style had created a climate in which students similar to Peter Daly experienced extreme difficulty in learning. The fact that questions were encouraged was positive. However, the directive manner in which the questions were answered did not permit collegial learning which Peter, and others, like him, needed. This teacher, though able and caring, was unable—or unwilling—to alter his teaching procedures. Although he was more than willing to give additional assistance to Peter, the way in which the sessions were held were carbon copies of his classroom approach. Thus, with Mr. Caputo, Peter could never achieve the grades that he was accustomed to receiving in all other courses. While the offering of assistance was important, Peter gained little from it.

Peter fared well in courses conducted in a different manner. He was a highly motivated and extremely responsible student. He had many friends and was a leading member of the school's cross country, track and field teams. He had no learning difficulties, but preferred collegial teachers who could present lessons deductively and globally as well as analytically. He did not think "in words," but, rather, was creative and thought "in pictures" that developed relationships. For this type of student, changes in instructor or course, if necessary, are critical *before* a mismatch in learning and teaching styles occurs. Timing is critical to reduce poor or failing results with all of their continuing negative consequences.

GUIDELINES

1. Every effort should be made to match teaching and learning styles.
2. Options should be explored before mismatches are scheduled, e.g., team-teaching, independent study, alternative courses and programs, out-of-school learning, paired sections with different teaching styles, and so on.
3. In-service training should be offered to build awareness of and ability to use the different styles responsive to individual students.
4. A student's ability to cope with different instructional styles and to learn by using his/her own strengths should be among the goals established by guidance counselors when working with youngsters.

REFERENCES

For verification of the importance of matching learning and teaching styles see the following:

1. Ronnie W. Copenhaver, "The Consistency of Student Learning Styles As Students Move From English to Mathematics," Ed.D. Dissertation, Indiana University (1979) which evidenced that: (a) students' learning styles remain consistent across subject areas; (b) students have significantly more positive attitudes toward classes when their and their teachers' styles are congruent; (c) a wide range of learning styles exists among students in any given class; and (d) many different teaching styles are necessary if instructors are to respond to the diversity of learning styles among their students.

2. Elsie Cafferty, "An Analysis of Student Performance Based Upon the Degree of Match Between the Educational Cognitive Style of the Teacher and the Educational Cognitive Style of the Students," Ed.D. Dissertation, University of Nebraska (1980) where the closer the match between the styles of students and their teachers, the higher the youngsters' grade point average; the more dissonant the match, the *lower* the grade point average.

3. Claudia B. Douglass, "Making Biology Easier to Understand," *The American Biology Teacher* 41, 5 (May, 1979) : 277-299.

4. Paul Trautman, "An Investigation of the Relationships Between Selected Instructional Techniques and Identified Cognitive Style," Ed.D. Dissertation, St. John's University (1979), both of which reported that when instructional *resources* are matched correctly with individual students' learning styles, statistically significant increases in academic achievement result; when they are mismatched, achievement levels *decrease*.

8
Leading Staff and Community in Instructional Improvement

SITUATION 36

> PROBLEM: Reviewing and Improving the Curriculum
>
> SITUATION: Committee Meeting

by
Josephine Gemake

Ms. Jones, the principal of School #16, realized that she had not seen any social studies being taught on her recent tour of the building. The weekly plan books reflected behavioral objectives in the area, but as she flipped through several of these books to see how the lessons were being planned, it was evident that the teachers had written repetitive objectives. She had seen no diorama exhibits in the showcases or projects on bulletin boards related to social studies. Indeed, while questions were posed at the monthly faculty conferences in reading and math, no one sought information pertaining to the mandated social studies curriculum.

She walked to the files and removed the summary sheets that reported the standardized test scores in social studies. The elementary school was located in an urban, blue-collar area and reported sixty-nine percent of its students reading at or above grade level. The mean and median for the standardized test scores in social studies were lower than those for the reading scores and reflected considerably poorer test performance. Ms. Jones questioned the lower scores in that area and decided to plan a monthly faculty conference around that curriculum. She jotted down the standardized test data and some comments about the trends she had observed in the lesson planning and made a note on her calendar to discuss the situation with the Curriculum Committee.

The Curriculum Committee had as members six teachers (one from each grade) and two parents. The staff of thirty-six had elected the Committee which met every third Wednesday from 2:00 P.M. to 3:00 P.M. when class coverage was less difficult to arrange. At its next meeting, Ms. Jones presented her data concerning the social studies test scores and her observations about the cursory lesson planning, and allowed time for members to discuss her comments. Two of the teachers admitted that they did not like to teach the social studies curriculum because the topics were not relevant to their students' interests. One teacher criticized the content of the commercial materials that had been supplied to teach the curriculum. Two of the group stated that they were not certain how to develop lessons in that area. After viewpoints and feelings were expressed, the remaining time was used to develop a brief questionnaire that was distributed among the faculty to determine staff needs in social studies.

When the results of the questionnaires were summarized, it was evident that each grade level had specific concerns about teaching that curriculum. The majority agreed that the content, skills and attitudes developed in the mandated course of study had to be redefined in terms of the current student population. Once the curriculum was reshaped, commercial materials suited to the new objectives could be ordered. Several teachers had indicated their need for retraining; thus, demonstration lessons and/or workshops had to be included in the revision planning. Ms. Jones anticipated few problems in soliciting parent and central office approval for the new curriculum, since the teachers would utilize the broad scope and sequence of concepts, skills and objectives as delineated by the mandated curriculum.

KEY ISSUES

A. How does a principal become aware of curriculum areas that require improvement?
B. How does he or she communicate this need and build awareness and a climate for change?
C. Which strategies should be employed to involve all in meaningful change?

ANALYSIS

At the monthly faculty conference, Ms. Jones presented the results of the questionnaires and explained the Committee's plans to reshape the social studies curriculum. It was estimated that a minimum of five months and five grade conferences would be necessary to accomplish that goal; a flexible schedule was established for curriculum development.

Grade Conference One:	Planning for revision to include establishing broad objectives, choosing topics for emphasis, collecting appropriate materials to use as resources, discussion and distribution of an outline to follow in writing the new curriculum.
Grade Conference Two:	Compilation, presentation and discussion of revised curriculum units; review of curriculum from other grades to ensure articulation and flow.
Grade Conference Three:	Presentation of sample lessons for inclusion in the curriculum.
Grade Conference Four:	Presentation of pre- and posttests for each unit.
Grade Conference Five:	Final review of the social studies curriculum for each grade.

Since three-fourths of the faculty had taught at School #16 for more than ten years, the teachers had definite ideas for curriculum changes and implementation. Discomfort with the current curriculum and the knowledge that they could reshape it to better respond to student interests provided motivation for their efforts.

After faculty approval was elicited, the Curriculum Committee met and designed a simple outline to be followed in format development. That provided a standardized structure within and between grades.

Each group was responsible for reviewing the respective curriculum assigned to that grade, with the chores for rewriting equally shared by the teachers. Each teacher chose a social studies unit to revise. As an example, the fifth grade studied economic geography. In order to understand economic interdependence and growth, several countries were compared and contrasted (i.e., United States/ Canada, Mexico/Brazil, Egypt/Nigeria, Germany/U.S.S.R. and India/Japan). Each teacher on that level identified specific goals, content objectives, skill objectives and suggestions for integration into other subject areas for the pair of countries chosen. The format for revision designed by the School Committee was followed.

A Teacher's Resource Shelf was established in the school library. Several teachers contacted friends who taught in other school districts and requested copies of their social studies curricula. A file of social studies curricula from other districts was compiled. The school librarian listed relevant materials available from the school library. Those materials were placed on the Resource Shelf. Some teachers were enrolled in graduate courses at local colleges; they borrowed curricula from the college libraries and made those materials available to others. A parent volunteer who was in charge of the school's Resource Room, was given a list of publishing companies to write to for sample materials.

Ms. Jones spoke at the Parent Association meeting and presented the plans for curriculum revision. Grade Leaders attended the meeting and briefly outlined the changes that would occur at each level. Parents approved the concept of revision with the understanding that they would see and comment on the final draft. They were encouraged to submit ideas and suggestions, and several volunteered to type. Because money for materials was limited, Ms. Jones asked the Parent Association to consider sponsoring a fund-raising drive for additional money for materials. The organization agreed to discuss that suggestion at its next meeting. The greatest burden of work occurred during the first two months of revision. Teachers rewrote the curriculum units assigned to them according to the designated outline, compiled, presented and reviewed the curriculum for their grade levels, and checked the sequential development of topics and skills from one level to the next. That was done during prep periods, and regular faculty meetings and, in many cases, on their own time because of interest and the equitable division of labor.

Because the teachers had requested training in the area of social studies, demonstration lessons were planned and developed during the third month of revision. Since there was a portable video recorder and tape machine available in the school, Ms. Jones asked that one teacher from each grade write and teach a brief demonstration lesson in the area of social studies. Each taped segment was no longer than ten minutes and illustrated a specific skill that could be developed through a social studies lesson. The six tapes were viewed and discussed at the grade conferences, and positive support and feedback were offered to the staff members who had pioneered their development.

Each teacher also was asked to contribute at least one lesson plan from each unit. In that way, a series of sample lessons for teaching the units was compiled; those were always selected from areas of strength to promote confidence and willingness to share.

Some teachers were willing to work together in pairs to develop the curriculum. They brought their classes together each Tuesday and Thursday. On Tuesday, while one teacher taught a social studies lesson to the two combined classes, the other teacher observed and assisted. The roles were reversed on Thursday. In that way, those who requested help in planning and teaching were provided support.

At grade conference #4, pre- and posttests for each unit were presented as evaluations. Objective questions of multiple choice and matching column types were written for each topic by the teacher who revised the unit. The pre- and posttest questions paralleled those asked in the annual standardized tests. In that way, increases in student achievement could be assessed, and test-taking behavior could be practiced at the same time.

At grade conference #5, the completed curriculum (goals, objectives, materials, areas of integration, pre- and posttest evaluations and sample lessons) was reviewed by each grade. Since the teachers were involved in teaching the curriculum as it was being developed, their suggestions for change were viable and practical.

It had taken six months to revise the curriculum. Some efforts were more complete than others. Ms. Jones began to see sequential development in lesson planning, and dioramas, displays and projects involving social studies topics were displayed. She hoped that the scores on the social studies tests would improve. Many teachers were enthusiastic about the new curriculum and used the sample plans in their daily lessons; only a few returned to their laissez-faire attitude. All, however, were aware of the new curriculum and the changes and had a more secure grasp of teaching methods.

GUIDELINES

1. Observe teacher planning and instruction in depth—from daily plans to what happens in the classroom; from students' work to their individual test scores; from what is said

about a curriculum area to actual teacher and student performance.
2. Establish respected teacher committees, with parent involvement when appropriate, to review, plan and involve all in necessary revision.
3. Seek long-range motivation through felt needs and accomplishment.
4. Provide time, assistance and support for serious, in-depth changes.

SITUATION 37

PROBLEM: Retraining Faculty

SITUATION: Case Study

by
Josephine Gemake

Mr. Smith, principal of the Woodlawn Elementary School, received a notice from the District Office that the State Education Department would begin to test for minimum competency in reading. Certain passing scores had been assigned for each grade level and students who could not achieve these would be retained. The reading test, developed by the State Education Department, employed a novel "holistic" technique for measuring comprehension of prose passages. Students would be required to read nonfiction paragraphs from which several words had been deleted and to select the appropriate words to complete the selections. Reading ability would be determined through the use of a unique unit of measure.

Reading approaches used at the Woodlawn Elementary School were sequentially analytic, and the skills that the students mastered could not be transferred to the new test format without specific instructions. The school's Curriculum Committee had chosen a phonics approach to use in the primary grades "... so that the students would have a foundation in word attack skills." Students in the middle grades were taught reading comprehension through a traditional basal reading approach. In the upper grades the students transferred those skills into an individualized literature program where they read what they chose at their own pace.

That highly organized reading approach represented a system through which seventy percent of the students in that lower socioeconomic, working-class community, were reading on or above grade level and with which the majority of the twenty-seven teachers who comprised the staff was comfortable. Eighty percent of the faculty had taught at the Woodlawn School for more than ten years and was stable, conservative and routinized. Changes in programs and methodology frequently were met with distrust, apathy and/or passive resistance.

Despite that potentially negative climate, Mr. Smith knew that he had to retrain his teaching staff to administer, score, interpret and evaluate the mandated statewide reading test. He also had to prepare them to instruct students in the strategies necessary to perform the reading comprehension tasks required by the new test. To add to his difficulty, the District Office had reported that no money was available for in-service training, and, therefore, no district-level workshops would be planned. Any in-service training that was deemed necessary would be the responsibility of each school administrator. Furthermore, no additional money for materials would be allocated; only State Education Department materials pertaining to the test could be distributed to the schools.

KEY ISSUES

A. Should a school be required to respond to state mandated changes in testing?
B. What are appropriate strategies for initiating change among stable, veteran teachers?
C. How can change be accomplished without additional funds for consultants, college tuition, in-service workshops or special materials?

ANALYSIS

Mr. Smith reasoned that monthly faculty conferences could be used for teacher training and that it was possible that staff members who had been enrolled in graduate programs had learned about the "holistic" approach to reading and could be used as resource people. By involving his staff in planning and implementing training sessions, he hoped to ensure cooperation and overcome resistance.

He posted the notice about the reading competency examination on the staff bulletin board and invited anyone who knew about that technique, and who would be willing to participate in planning and presenting faculty conferences on the topic, to sign his/her name on a sheet attached to the notice. Five teachers indicated that they had background and had received training in that particular reading technique. Mr. Smith arranged for those teachers to be released from classes and met with them to plan three faculty conferences, each of which would be limited to one hour in length. Objectives for each conference were delineated, and content and materials were designed to meet them. The planning group also developed a simple questionnaire to evaluate the training sessions.

The first conference presented an overview of the new reading method and provided the teachers with a "hands-on" experience. The conference planning team devised a mock reading test that followed the format of the new state reading test. Teachers were asked to respond to the test items and to be aware of the strategies they used in answering each question. The techniques that mature readers used in arriving at the correct answers were discussed and examined, and suggestions for teaching those strategies to students were elicited.

The second conference used the planning team and teacher trainers to demonstrate lessons and materials that could be used in working with students. Publishers of those reading programs used in the school had been contacted, and one had sent free samples of printed materials which then were distributed to staff members. Each teacher was asked to develop reading materials suitable for the students in his/her class. Those materials were collected by the grade leaders and sent to the General Office for reproduction and distribution. In that way, each teacher had a range of varied materials at different levels from which to plan and work. Mr. Smith announced that he expected those lessons and materials to be included in the weekly plan books.

A guest speaker was invited to address the third faculty meeting. One teacher had taken a graduate course at a local college with a professor who was active in community affairs and who consented to lead a discussion on test score interpretation and evaluation. She brought with her new ideas and materials for lessons.

A "Comment Box" had been set up in the General Office. Teachers were asked to jot down questions, ideas and feelings as they occurred while working in the new area of reading. Time was taken at each meeting to respond to those comments.

A reference library pertaining to the theory, testing techniques and materials for training in holistic reading was established. The school library subscribed to some professional journals, and the librarian was asked to research, compile and distribute a list of articles on the topic. The teachers on the planning committee volunteered textbooks, bibliographies and samples of pertinent materials which were circulated through the school library.

Before the test date arrived, Mr. Smith's staff had learned to teach and test for reading comprehension in the new way. Some teachers continued to integrate their learning into daily reading lessons. Others trained students in those reading techniques only at test time. The teachers completed the questionnaires designed to evaluate the training sessions in which they had participated. Through the responses of the faculty, Mr. Smith would be able to improve future teacher training sessions.

GUIDELINES

1. Involve staff directly in: (a) changes that affect the way they teach; (b) planning how the change will occur (in-service training during faculty meetings in this case); (c) who will take responsibility (the volunteer planning group); and (d) peer training and reaction (demonstration lessons, teacher-made materials and suggestions).
2. Seek assistance from publishers, colleges, the Central Office, other schools and the staff itself.
3. Follow-up with staff feedback, supervision and ongoing faculty-designed training sessions.

SITUATION 38

PROBLEM: Involving Students in Cocurricular Activities

SITUATION: Newspaper Article

by
Shirley A. Griggs

Phil Head was upset at first because the big city media to the north elected to focus on a story printed in his high school newspaper, *The Siren*. As he reread it, however, the principal recognized that this added spotlight, no matter how uncomfortable for him and the school, would probably awaken citizens and the Board from the darkness of apathetic self-delusion about the drugs their kids were taking and sharing. He posted the story near his office; he knew the teachers had it on the bulletin board in their lounge; the *New York Metro* was sold out around town, too. Phil underlined the headline and read it again:

School Playground Test for State's Tough Shield Law

It was the kind of story most young reporters dream about covering; a banner front page exclusive about a drug dealer, known only as the "Bon-Bon Man," who sold "ludes, pot, speed, black beauties and special hash to any student who could afford them, even fifth graders."

When it ran in the Shelton Senior High School *Siren* this month, the article carried no byline because the newspaper's faculty adviser, Harry Sherman, feared the student reporter would be the victim of reprisals from drug dealers and users. Yesterday, as the story triggered a dispute over the rights of the press and the prerogatives of the law, Mr. Sherman said he would protect the reporter's anonymity even if it meant going to jail.

Mr. Sherman also said that the story was intended to publicize the drug problem at the Shelton schools. Soon after it appeared, the County Prosecutor, M. T. Bookbinder, subpoenaed Mr. Sherman to tell a grand jury the name of the student reporter who had interviewed the "Bon-Bon Man" in the hope that the youngster would lead the authorities to the dealer. When Sherman, a fifty-eight-year-old social studies teacher refused, the prosecutor went to court.

This state has one of the nation's toughest Shield Laws, one that protects news organizations from being forced to disclose confidential sources except under specific circumstances. However, Superior Court Judge Imma Medlin ruled that the law didn't apply to *The Siren* because the newspaper wasn't published weekly, didn't have a paid circulation and wasn't registered with the postal service as second class matter. And, while the First Amendment protects the right of a student paper to publish, just as it does a commercial one, Judge Medlin ruled that it otherwise did not apply in this case. The judge said that if Mr. Bookbinder's investigators cannot discover who the "Bon-Bon Man" is by Thursday, he will order Mr. Sherman to name the student reporter. If that occurred, Sherman said he would appeal.

KEY ISSUES

A. Should school newspapers, clubs and other organizations become involved in real and often sensitive and controversial local and social issues?

B. What role should the principal play as head of the school, supervisor of all student activities and potential censor of student output in these areas?

C. How should the principal advise faculty and students who become embroiled in controversial situations?

D. What programs can the principal establish to combat the spreading use of drugs?

ANALYSIS

Problems and controversies can develop around other aspects of the student activities program, including the rights, responsibilities, and limitations of student government, the cliques and special student interest groups that are fostered and promoted through some school clubs and the emphasis upon competition as opposed to involvement in relation to the athletic program.

The mandate for the school principal is to foster a student activities program that provides youth with opportunities to be responsible, caring and involved members of our society while diminishing the possibilities of such involvement resulting in (a) cliques and polarization of students and faculty, or (b) irresponsible actions that are ultimately harmful to others.

Certainly, the advantages of establishing a viable, comprehensive student activities program far outweigh the disadvantages. The purposes of such a program should be to meet the school-related interests and needs of students that are not provided for in the curricular program and to provide realistic cocurricular experiences.

Possible special objectives of the student activities program are to help students:

- learn to use leisure time more productively;
- increase and use constructively the unique talents and skills they possess in realistic situations;
- develop new vocational, avocational and recreational interests;
- develop positive attitudes toward self and others;
- participate in a group or team approach to achievement, productivity or recreational activity; and
- develop more positive attitudes toward school and community.

The student activities program should be designed to serve the needs of all students, not just the more active and talented ones. Additionally, the various components of the program should not foster cliques or reinforce segregation on the basis of class or ethnic-racial differences; eligibility requirements should be flexible and relatively open.

In the situation of the anonymous reporter who interviewed the "Bon-Bon Man," the principal and faculty advisor followed all legal avenues available, based on constitutional rights, to protect their beliefs. Naturally, a final court of appeals ruling would be recognized by the central figures, whichever way the decision went.

In any event, the school and the community have been forced to confront an apparently serious drug situation. Investigations, counter-programs and student and professional involvement must be initiated. The co-curricular activity involving the school newspaper certainly met several of the program's objectives.

GUIDELINES

1. Each activity in a co-curricular program should have well-defined, written objectives.
2. The director of each activity should be a well-qualified, interested faculty advisor.
3. Written role descriptions should exist for the student officers of each activity.
4. An in-service program should be scheduled each year to help student officers improve their leadership skills.
5. A complete, written description of the total student activities program should be disseminated to students at the beginning of the school year.

The overall student activities program and each of its components should be evaluated periodically to ascertain effectiveness and to identify areas that need improvement.

SITUATION 39

> PROBLEM: Obtaining Public Input and Acceptance
>
> SITUATION: The Telephone Campaign

by
Shirley A. Griggs

Mrs. Teiten was extremely concerned when she called her friend, Mrs. Fowler.

"I'm so upset. Last night my twelve-year-old daughter asked me if I practiced birth control. After questioning her, I learned that the sixth graders in her school are required to take a sex education class. In looking over her classroom materials, I found that they are very explicit in terms of explaining and illustrating physical sex, various methods of birth control and even the abortion issue. My daughter is too young to handle this type of sex education."

Mrs. Fowler gasped, "That's shocking! My son, Bob, is only ten, and I certainly don't want him learning that kind of thing in school. When the time comes, my husband will take him aside and talk with him. Sex education should be a matter for the home and church, not the school. I intend to talk to the principal and get Bob excused from that class when the time comes. And I think we should get our friends to complain to the Board of Education."

KEY ISSUES

    A. When schools confront gaps in education in areas previously dealt with by parents, should the principal recommend:

1. a traditional curriculum?
2. a selected "bandwagon" approach?
3. new curriculum courses as electives? and/or
4. involvement by parents and the community in curriculum decisions?

B. Should schools consider interaction with the community on such subjects as:
1. sex education;
2. psychological education;
3. moral development;
4. death education;
5. substance abuse prevention; and/or
6. values clarification?

C. How can a principal deal with community objections to courses already in place?

ANALYSIS

With recent increases in teenage pregnancies, adolescent suicides and alcohol and drug abuse, schools have identified a need to expand the curriculum in an effort to deal with such problems and concerns. As a result, the secondary school curriculum now frequently includes courses in sensitive and controversial areas such as sex education, psychological education, moral development, death education, substance abuse prevention and values clarification.

The school administrator has a number of options regarding this type of new curriculum.

1. *Maintain the traditional curriculum.* The recent interest in setting academic standards in terms of minimum competency requirements for graduation is a development that has placed increased importance on the traditional curriculum; i.e., reading, social studies, English, science, writing and mathematics. States that have mandated minimum competency requirements for graduation generally have established checkpoints at various earlier grade levels in the school system to insure that student academic progress is on target. A case can be made by a school system that takes the position that it "cannot be all things to all students." Priorities must be established, and the academic curriculum becomes a primary concern; affective education is secondary.

2. *Adopt the "get on the bandwagon" approach.* The educational literature is replete with descriptions of many model or exemplary programs and courses. Additionally, the programs and workshops at local, state and national professional education conventions offer information on the latest curricular emphases, trends and innovations. Too often, little effort is involved in designing and implementing such programs; consideration must be given to the special needs of each local school population and the desires or concerns of its parent/community groups.

3. *Establish the new curriculum as elective, not required, courses.* Secondary students have different levels of ability, aptitude and interest, and the overall curriculum should be responsive to those variations. The trend among college admission requirements has been away from mandated courses at the secondary level, such as Latin, English literature or trigonometry and toward broad acceptance of electives in specific discipline areas. Additionally, the moral values of parents must be considered before mandating courses in sensitive areas like sex education, where it is difficult to teach content apart from values.

4. *Involve parents and the community in curriculum decision-making.* Most parents want opportunities to become involved with their children's school, particularly in a decision-making capacity. Parent involvement can take many forms ranging from total community control of educational policy to informational participation via the media and newsletters. It is generally recognized that there is a fundamental need to bring parents and the neighboring community into closer relationship with the school. Home support is essential if children are to learn effectively in school.

Option 4, involving parents and community citizens in decisions regarding curriculum development, seems to be the most desirable. Provide opportunities for both individual parents and parent/community groups to express their desires, identify their concerns, ask questions and become involved in determinations concerning the school program.

GUIDELINES

1. Establish a school (and district) curriculum committee consisting of parents designated by a PTA or other school community group, teachers, supervisors, the principal and Central Office administrators.

2. Involve parents on a broad basis to become informed, to react, to provide feedback on programs and to develop new organizational plans and projected new courses at meetings designed to include them in the decision-making process.
3. Use survey instruments, needs assessments and brainstorming sessions to set goals and to establish priorities and evaluation criteria.

SITUATION 40

PROBLEM: Exhibiting Leadership Qualities

SITUATION: The Faculty Meeting

by
Kathy Shanahan

A warm breeze blew gently through the opened classroom windows—a breeze that seemed to whisper, "Summer is here." The Wednesday faculty meeting was about to begin. The usual good-natured, give-and-take atmosphere that preceded all meetings was replaced by low, private conversations. Anxiety hung like a nervous cloud over the room.

Earlier that morning, a note had been circulated by the principal stating simply that, with the faculty's permission, the approved agenda would be postponed to a future date. Instead, a matter of grave importance to all would be explored and shared.

The principal opened the meeting by reading excerpts from Martin Luther King's, "I Have a Dream." After a time for quiet meditation, he nodded and said, "We have trouble right here in River City."

For the next ten minutes the principal spoke softly and sensitively, addressing a problem that she sensed was very evident—faculty negativism. She continually emphasized that the teacher's role as educator in this particular school was perhaps more difficult than in most others. "You are dealing with children who are the product of a culture that is very different from your own. Their socioeconomic background influences their values and priorities toward goals that are different from ours."

At the completion of her discourse, she stated that no promises could be made that current difficulties would be ameliorated. It was suggested that the teachers survey their own attitudes and perhaps "channel them" to make possible feelings of personal reward and satisfaction. The principal offered a few practical suggestions for them to try in their classrooms:

1. temporarily dropping the regular curriculum;
2. seeking light, motivating activities based on interests;
3. using the outdoors for instruction on warm days;
4. picnicking with the children;
5. finding humorous situations; enjoying the children;
6. sharing with "up" people when you felt "down";
7. changing teaching styles to match the way in which these individuals learned best; for example, using tactual/kinesthetic games and materials;
8. allowing the students the opportunities to create some of the ways in which they would learn, such as building and designing their own teaching materials to use with other students.

The meeting ended, and the faculty left in a relatively jovial mood with the exception of two or three who departed sheepishly, their heads down.

The remainder of the month proved to be calm. Most teachers took to heart the principal's advice and managed to maintain a positive climate through the hectic last days of the year—with one problem: two teachers resigned during the last days of school.

The resignations came within one day of each other. The two accused the principal of having reprimanded them in front of the entire faculty at the meeting in which she had talked of negativism. They further stated that it would have been more beneficial if she had spoken about their deficits in the privacy of her office rather than openly. The principal informed those teachers that the "pep talk" was not directed toward any single teacher in particular, but, rather, to the entire staff, because of the continuing apathy in the building.

After the resignations, the principal discussed the validity of her approach with each member of the faculty, all of whom reassured her that her strategy had been appropriate. Negativism was contagious. Many members of the staff admitted they had succumbed. Most agreed that it had been helpful having the administration bring the problem to the surface.

KEY ISSUES

A. What is the best approach for overcoming general apathy and negativism?
B. How does a principal deal with individual faculty members whose negativism adversely affects their effectiveness as teachers?
C. Should there be differences in the principal's strategy when dealing with tenured and nontenured teachers? With contract teachers in a nonpublic school?

ANALYSIS

Negativism or apathy are problems that many teachers experience. Before solutions can be worked out, individuals must be aware that a problem exists, admit it and discover its source. Awareness is the critical step. The willingness to admit the problem is essential to its solution. It is hoped that the discovery of the source will result in finding feasible methods to confront and overcome the difficulty. Allowing the cause of the problem to remain undefined only results in finding superficial remedies that are usually short-lived.

Groups of teachers may lapse into negativism as they attempt to work together in a difficult situation. In this case, the administrator realized the problem existed and identified its source—the type of youngster they were teaching.

It may be difficult for an administrator to admit that his or her faculty is operating with a defeatist attitude. It's even more difficult to confront the faculty with that type of problem. This administrator exercised leadership by taking the initiative and discussing the problem openly. Once awareness was established, positive action could be taken.

This administrator was also on target in defining the cause—the difficulties encountered when working with those particular children—children who came from a community that was experiencing deterioration and economic hardships.

Focusing on a single, important topic with the faculty can be invigorating, positive and beneficial in building dynamic and cohesive group action. Knowing the faculty, selecting the right time and deciding which important issues warrant an entire meeting are critical aspects of the principal's planning and decision-making in this approach.

Follow-up conferences with individual faculty members are essential to continuing action on the problem.

One disturbing aspect of this case was the resignation of two teachers shortly after the discussion of negativism. Individuals who were not performing on an acceptable level should have had observations and meetings with the principal and other supervisors long before the last month of school. That would be true of probationary teachers in the public school system or contract teachers in nonpublic schools. Tenured teachers who lapse into extreme negativism or apathy should receive early assistance too, in a form that addresses their needs, such as released time, transfer of students or class assignments, positive, motivating responsibilities, advice on personal problems, peer counseling, higher-order tasks, stress and burnout sessions, and so on.

Whether at an open session or at later, follow-up meetings, the principal should be open, positive, sincere, receptive, supportive and ready to plan and to take action on various professional suggestions that come from the staff. Faculty members should feel free to voice their feelings, perceptions and positive suggestions. Collaborative leadership will tend to dispel negativism and permit solutions to most problems.

GUIDELINES

1. Confront problems with individual teachers as soon as they surface; work directly with the people concerned.
2. Know the values, personalities, likely reactions of the individuals on the faculty and how they function as a group. A

group is a different entity than the sum of its individual parts.
3. Select the right issues and the right time to bring a problem to the entire faculty.
4. Involve the faculty in the solution of the problems if they perceive or are convinced that the issues are important to them.
5. Provide assistance in the form of alternative training, counseling, resources, changes, rewards, responsibilities, projects, transfers or whatever is professionally appropriate in solving a specific problem.

Index

A

Acceptance, obtaining, 213–216
Accreditation, regional, 185–189
Achievement, result of maturity, 84
Achievement scores, 28
Action plan, desegregation, 111–112
Activities, student, 126–131
Administrative council, 22
Advisory committee, student, 110
Advisory groups, curriculum, 69–73
Aides, parent, 98
Alternative courses and programs, 196
Articles, school paper, 127, 129
Assistant principals:
  cafeteria observations, 108
  chain of command, 92–96
  complaints, 96
  delegating tasks, 117–123
  desegregation, 108–112 (*see also* Desegregation)
  determine heart of issue, 96
  funding, 117–123
  instructional effectiveness, 97–107
  listening to students, 113–117
  memos, meeting, reports, 117–123
  objective, 96
  requests, 96
  suggestions, 96
  taking charge, 97–107
  teachers' room ultimatum, 92–96
  understanding of goals, 96
Attendance:
  effect of extra activites, 46–49
  grades, 61–63
  teacher, 92
Attitude:
  authoritarian, 75
  desegregation, 111
  development, 47
  grades, 62, 63
  "new broom" superintendent, 21
  new program, 27–31, 55–60, 81–89
Authoritarian attitude, 75, 181

B

Behavior:
  adult, 41–42, 101–106
  cheating, 74–78
  child, 41–42
  effective instructional environment, 40–43
  grades, 63
  individualization, 101–107
  interpersonal, 83
  new superintendent, 20
  nonconforming, 100
  outcomes, 101–106
  overly conforming, 83
  pubescent, 131
  rebel, 137–144
  student, 101–107
Bias, desegregation, 109 (*see also* Desegregation)
Biographical data, 21
Board of Education:
  attendance and grades, 61–63
  divided or misguided members, 52–54
  members administer building, 49–51
  negotiations sabotage, 52–54
  occupational program, 61–63
  planning for visits, 55–60
  policy decisions, 46–49
  program value dispute, 46–49
  reaching goals for students, 46–49
  schools and other educational units, 61–63
  timely phone call, 52–54
  visits and confrontations, 49–51
  where the action is, 55–60
Budget:
  approvals, 28
  priorities, 51
  salary increase, 52–54
Burnout, teacher:
  avoiding, 164
  causes, 165–166
  definition, 163–164
  faculty views, 165

Burnout, teacher *(cont'd)*
  parents, 164, 165
  prevention, 166–167
  rewards, 164
  small class sizes, 165
  standards for students, 164
  stress, 165, 166
  symptoms, 164, 165
  urban teachers, 165
  values, 165
  younger teachers, 165

C

Campaigns, school, 46
Carbo, 32
Careers:
  guidance, 25
  minorities, 109
Caucus, monthly, 22
Censorship, Student Council, 127
Central office:
  domineering ombudsman, 23–27
  goals, district administrators, 37–43
  gossip, 18–22
  initiating mandated program, 27–31
  "new broom" superintendent, 18–22
  new principal, 37–43
  phase-in of program, 27–30
  responding to direction, 31–36
  teacher and student, 23–27
  using professional consultants, 31–36
Chain of command, 92–96, 131–137
Challenge Program, 82–88
Change:
  deciding, 22
  design teams at top, 185–189
  managing the process, 175–197
  mismatching teacher and student, 194–197
  needed, 70
  program, 27–31
  promoted by principal, 70
  regional accreditation, 185–189
  students' rights, 176–179
  supervisory decisions, 194–197
  time and priorities, 180–185
  visiting classrooms is only part, 190–193
Cheating, 74–78
Cheerleaders, 131–137
Classroom, 98–99, 158
Class size, 165

Closed Door policy, 180–184
Clubs, 46–49, 117, 126
Cocurricular activities, 46–49, 209–212
College-bound students, 25–26
College entrance assistance, 26
Command, chain, 92–96, 131–137
Committee, sounding board, 22
Communication, workshops, 112
Communication in action, 111
Communication training, 111
Community:
  cheating by students, 74–78
  curriculum advisory groups, 69–73
  early reading program, 69–73
  enlisting cooperation, 65–89
  griping at new program, 81–89
  hasty decisions, 66–68
  parental pressure, 66–68
  PTA, 78–80
  written complaints, 74–78
Competency exam, 148–152, 205–208
Competitions, 46–49
Complaints, written, 74–78
Confidential information, 52–54
Conformity, 63
Consultants:
  hostility toward, 28
  professional, 31–36
Contests, 46–49
Contract Activity Packages, 158
Contracts, 99
Contributions of minority children, 109
Counseling:
  group, 111–112
  minorities, 109
  personalized, 27
Counselor, guidance, 25
Course completion, 63
Courses, guidance, 27
Creative arts, 100
Curriculum:
  advisory groups, 69–73
  instructional improvement, 199–220 (*see also* Instruction)
  public input and acceptance, 213–216
  reviewing and improving, 200–205
  social studies, 200–205

D

Decisions:
  early reading program, 69–73
  hasty, principal, 66–68

INDEX

Decisions *(cont'd)*
  instructional goals, 47
  making, 83
  parents and community, 215
  principal, 20
  punitive action, 67–68
  supervisory, right time, 194–197
Delegation, higher order tasks, 117–123
Demonstration lessons, 97, 201
Desegregation:
  academics, 112
  access to resources, 110
  action plan, 111
  attitudes, 108, 111
  awareness and communication, 112
  awareness of racial stereotypes, 111
  behavior patterns, 108
  biased discipline, 109
  career opportunities, 109
  classroom, 110
  classroom practices, 109
  classrooms based on ability, 108
  cocurricular areas, 112
  cocurricular clubs, 108
  communication in action, 111
  communicaiton training, 111
  conditions promoting integration, 109
  contributions of minority children, 109
  counseling practices, 109
  cultural fairness, 110
  desegregated classes together, 110
  discussions at faculty meetings, 110
  early grades, 110
  "educational" practices, 108
  essential program elements, 109
  expectations for performance, 109
  feelings, 111
  field trips, 110
  follow-up to action plan, 112
  goal-setting, 112
  group counseling, 111–112
  grouping, 109
  human relations workshops, 110
  institutional practices, 109
  instructional materials, 109
  integration through recreation, 111
  interethnic staff, 110
  lack of openness, 109
  learning, 112
  literature, 112
  majority student leadership, 109
  minority history course, 110
  minority student percentages, 110
  minority students as individuals, 109

Desegregation *(cont'd)*
  negative atmosphere, 109
  old methods, 108
  peer assistance, 112
  policies, 108
  post-secondary education, 109
  problem-solving, 112
  procedures, 108
  race and socioeconomic class, 110
  recent studies, 112
  representatives of goups, 112
  services, 110
  sports, 112
  student advisory committee, 110
  student interaction, 112
  summer planning sessions, 110
  teacher-student relationships, 109
  teaching styles, 108
  teaming, 112
  "test-score grouping," 110
  text materials, 110
Dioramas, 200
Disciplinary action:
  minorities, 109
  principal, 66–68
Discussions:
  class, 33
  small-group, 79
Door, open or closed, 180–184
Drugs, 138, 209–212

E

Elections, school, 46
Employability profiles, 63
Employability skills, 62
Enrichment activities, 82
Evaluation:
  ongoing, 49
  policies, 63
  teacher's performance, 160–163
Expectations, minorities, 109
Extracurricular activities, 46–49, 113–117

F

Faculty, retraining, 201, 202, 205–208
Faculty meetings, 78–80, 92, 101, 110, 216–220
Failure, competency exam, 148–152
Feelings, races, 111
Field trips, 110

Filby, 33
First Amendment, 126, 128, 130, 210
Fisher, 33
Freedom of press, 128
Frustration, teacher, 165, 167
Funding, sources, 117–123
Fund-raising activities, 126–131

G

Gifted students, 22, 49, 82–88
Goals:
    educational, policies, 48
    policy decisions, 46–49
    program, 22
    reaching ones for students, 46–49
    setting, 112
    setting with district administrators, 37–43
Gossip, 18–22
Government, student, 46
Grades:
    attendance, 62
    attitudes, 62, 63
    basis, 147
    behavior, 63
    conformity, 63
    consistent and fair, 147
    course completion, 63
    disputed, 144–147, 176–179
    employability profiles, 63
    employability skills, 62
    evaluation policies, 63
    make-up work, 63
    noncognitive concerns, 147
    not used as weapon, 147
    occupational program, 61–63
    performance on objectives, 62, 63
    philosophy, 62
    report cards, 62, 145–147
    rules, 62, 63
    students' rights, 176–179
Grievance, filing, 93, 160–162
Griping, new program, 81–89
Group discussions, 79
Grouping:
    minorities, 109
    reading, 72
    "test-score," 110
Group instruction, 159
Guidance:
    courses, 27

Guidance (cont'd)
    marginal student, 154–160
Guidance counselor, 25
Gym class, 146

H

Halls, 100
Handbook, student, 138
Harassment, 93
Health and Physical Education, 134, 135, 136
History, minority, 110
Homerooms, special, 117
Human relations field trips, 110
Human relations workshops, 110

I

Independent study, 196
Individual educational programs, 146
Individualization:
    adult behaviors, 101–107
    answers to questions, 100
    areas to improve, 104–106
    assignments on chalkboard, 100
    behavioral outcomes, 101–107
    behavioral patterns, 100
    charts, 99
    children interact freely, 99
    children tutoring each other, 100
    completing filmstrips, 99
    continual direction, 98
    creating games, 99
    creative arts, 100
    criteria and goals, 101
    crossword puzzles, 99
    demonstration lessons, 97
    different activities, 100
    discussions, 100
    dittos, 99
    excerpts of research, 159
    faculty meetings, 101
    hallways, 100
    in-service sessions, 97, 101, 159
    "instructional areas", 98–99
    mathematics games, 99
    needs of all children, 69, 70
    nonconformists, 100
    objectives on contracts, 99
    parents involved, 98
    positive observations, 101–103

INDEX

Reading *(cont'd)*
  kindergarten program, 69–73
  leisure, 22
  paraprofessional, 72, 73
  parent aides, 98
  parent volunteers, 72
  part-time person, 72
  phonics approach, 50
  raising state test scores, 31
  readiness materials, 73
  "Reading-for-Pleasure" program, 72
  selecting outside assistance, 33
  shared grouping, 72
  sight vocabulary, 71
  specialists, 70, 71, 72, 73
  speed and comprehension, 32
  test for minimum competency, 205–208
  time span when taught, 32
  "transition activities," 33
  visual discrimination, 71
Rebel, 137–144
Regional accreditation, 185–189
Released time from classes, 48
Remediation, 148–152
Report cards, 62, 145–147 (*see also* Grades)
Reporting to parents, 22
Research data, 51, 159
Resources, equal access, 110
Resource Shelf, Teacher's, 203
Resumés, 21
Retraining teachers, 201, 202, 205–208
Rumor, 18–22

S

Salary increase, 52–54
Scheduling, 78–80
School:
  major problems, 59–60
  recommendations, 59–60
  strengths and weaknesses, 58–59
School paper, 126–131, 209–212 (*see also* Paper, school)
Science, multi-age core, 82
Segregation (*see* Desegregation)
Services, 110
Shield Law, 209, 210
Singer, 32
Socioeconomic background, 111, 217
Sounding board committee, 22
Specialists, reading, 70, 71, 72, 73
Split-session kindergarten classes, 70

Sports, 112
Staff:
  interethnic, 110
  strengths and qualifications, 20
Stallings, 33
Standardized test scores, 200
Statistics, 41
Stereotypes, racial, 111
Stress, 166, 167
Student activities, 126–131
Student activities program, 211, 212
Student advisory committee, 110
Student Council:
  after-school organizations, 126
  autonomy of school paper, 128
  censorship, 127
  claim to authority, 126, 129, 130
  concern about articles, 129
  financial statements, 126, 130
  First Amendment, 126, 128, 130
  freedom of press, 128
  fund-raising activities, 126, 129, 130
  impact of administrative support, 129
  impotent, 127
  neutral administration, 129
  overzealous, 130
  past disinterest, 128
  power to penalize, 128
  regulating student activities, 129
  righteousness, 128
  rights upheld, 127, 130
  schoolwide constituency, 129
  student interest, 129
  uniting student body, 127, 130
  whether or not to exercise authority, 128
Student handbook, 138
Student interaction, 112
Student participation:
  bypassing chain of command, 131–137
  child study team, 148–152
  competency exam failed, 148–152
  disputed grade, 144–147
  protest, 126–131
  rebel without cause, 137–144
  school paper, 126–131 (*see also* Paper, school)
  Student Council, 126–131 (*see also* Student Council)
Students, marginal:
  diagnosis, 157
  individualized program, 158–160
  individual needs, 157
  instructional environment, 158

Students, marginal *(cont'd)*
    Learning Style Inventory, 157–158
    learning styles, 157–159
    monitoring progress, 158
    multisensory instructional resources, 158
    potential dropouts, 157, 159
    proposal to reach, 154–158
Student-teacher program, 78–80
Summer, planning sessions, 110
Superintendent, "new broom," 18–22
Supervisory decisions, 194–197

T

Talented, programs, 22
Teacher-Learning Situation, 42–43
Teachers, motivating:
    burnout, 163–167 *(see also* Burnout, teacher)
    improving performance, 167–171
    low morale, 171–174
    marginal students, 154–160 *(see also* Students, marginal)
    observing, evaluating, 160–163
    stress, 166, 167
    union, 160–163
    urban, 165
    younger, 165
Teachers' Union, 160–163
Teaming, desegregation, 112
Teams, 131–137
Teams at the top, 185–189
Team-teaching, 196
Telephone campaign, 213–216
Testing, programs or materials, 35
Text materials, multiethnic, 110
Time, planning, 180–185
Traditional school, 50
Training, re-, 201, 202, 205–208

U

Union, 160–163
Urban teachers, 165

V

Visits, 55–60, 160–162, 189, 190–193

W

Workshops, 51, 110, 112, 159, 166, 201
Writing skills, 22

Y

Younger teachers, 165